D0238181

The Human Givens Approach 'Essential help in Troubled Times' Series is a range of best-selling books, each of which explores a recognised psychological or behavioural problem and shows in clear, non-jargonistic language how to treat it effectively with psychological interventions.

How to master anxiety is the third title in the series which includes: *How to Lift Depression...fast; Freedom from Addiction: The secret behind successful addiction busting; How to Liberate Yourself from Pain;* and *Release from Anger.* (The series is part of a larger nationwide effort to move counselling, psychotherapy and education away from ideology and more into line with scientific findings about how the brain works and what people really need to live fulfilling lives.)

Joe Griffin is a research psychologist with graduate and post-graduate degrees from the LSE. He is hugely influential in the world of psychotherapy and is director of studies at the Human Givens Institute. He is co-author with Ivan Tyrrell of numerous best-selling titles including *Human Givens: A new approach to emotional health and clear thinking; How to lift depression... fast; Freedom from Addiction; Dreaming Reality: How dreaming keeps us sane or can drive us mad* and *Release from Anger*.

Ivan Tyrrell has worked for many years as a psychotherapist (specialising in brief therapy for depression and anxiety) and now spends most of his time lecturing and writing. For four-teen years he was Principal of MindFields College which taught a wide range of psychotherapeutic skills to health and welfare professionals (including psychotherapists, counsellors, social workers, psychologists, nurses, doctors, psychiatrists, teachers, youth workers, occupational therapists, NHS and social welfare staff) across the UK. He is editorial director of the Human Givens journal and a Director of the Human Givens Institute. As a result, his influence in (and knowledge of) the field of psychotherapy and counselling is considerable.

Denise Winn is a journalist specialising in psychology and medicine, and editor of the *Human Givens* journal.

How to master
anxiety

All you need to know to overcome
stress, panic attacks, phobias,
trauma, obsessions
and more

Change is much easier
than you think...

Joe Griffin & Ivan Tyrrell

with Denise Winn

ALSO BY THE AUTHORS

*Human Givens: A new approach to
emotional health and clear thinking*
Joe Griffin and Ivan Tyrrell

*Dreaming Reality: How dreaming
keeps us sane or can drive us mad*
Joe Griffin and Ivan Tyrrell

How to lift depression ... fast
Joe Griffin and Ivan Tyrrell

*Freedom from Addiction: The secret
behind successful addiction busting*
Joe Griffin and Ivan Tyrrell

*Release from Anger: Practical help
for controlling unreasonable rage*
Joe Griffin and Ivan Tyrrell

The Origin of Dreams
Joe Griffin

The Survival Option
Ivan Tyrrell

Editors/contributors to:

*An Idea in Practice: Using the
human givens approach*

How to master
anxiety

A practical handbook

PUBLISHING

Joe Griffin & Ivan Tyrrell

with Denise Winn

PUBLISHING

First published in Great Britain 2007
Reprinted 2007, 2008, 2010, 2011 and 2012

Copyright © Joe Griffin, Ivan Tyrrell and Denise Winn 2007

The right of Joe Griffin, Ivan Tyrrell and Denise Winn to be identified as the
authors of this work has been asserted in accordance with sections 77 and 78
of the Copyright, Designs and Patents Act 1988.

Published by HG Publishing, an imprint of Human Givens Publishing Ltd,
Chalvington, East Sussex, BN27 3TD, United Kingdom.
www.humangivens.com

A catalogue record for this book is available from the British Library.

ISBN 1-899398-81-3   ISBN-13 978-1-899398-81-2

All rights reserved. No part of this publication may be reproduced, stored in a
retrieval system, or transmitted in any form or by any means electronic,
mechanical, photocopying, recording, or otherwise, without the prior
written permission of the publishers.

Typeset in Book Antiqua and Conduit Condensed.
Printed and bound by CPI Group (UK) Ltd, Croydon, CR0 4YY.
Index by Indexing Specialists (UK) Ltd.

"Action conquers fear."

PROVERB

CONTENTS

Acknowledgements

We would like to thank Mark Bajer, Mike Beard,
Helen Card, Martin Murphy, Dr Farouk Okhai and
Pat Williams for contributing some of the case
histories used in this book, and our editor,
Jane Tyrrell, whose thoughtful work brought
greater clarity to the endeavour.

Taking back control

*I*T'S ONLY human to feel anxious ... some of the time. After all, it is part of our survival kit – none of us would live long if anxiety didn't stop us taking foolhardy risks. But too much anxiety can be problematic, as you are no doubt well aware, if you have chosen to pick up this book. When it gets out of control, anxiety can quickly become as disabling as any chronic physical illness.

Perhaps you have experienced overwhelming, unrealistic fears or worry, panic attacks, phobias, obsessive-compulsive behaviours or post-traumatic stress reactions that have stopped you from living your life as you would like to. All are examples of anxiety running riot, mentally and emotionally crippling us in the process, and a great many suffer from them. If this is how it is for you, or someone you care about, or your days are blighted by continual low-grade anxiety, it can feel as if life will never be normal again – as if something alien is in control.

But anxiety is *not* all-powerful and inexplicable. It can be managed very easily, when you know how.

And that is the point of this book. Whatever your own level or cause of anxiety, there are ways to overcome it. Having worked successfully for over 20 years with countless people, young and old, suffering from varying degrees and types of anxiety, we know from first-hand experience what a difference the information and techniques that you are about to read about make to people's lives.

> 66 Anxiety is not all powerful and inexplicable – it can be managed very easily ... when you know how. 99

Anxiety is made up of three elements: the physical sensations you experience, the emotions you have while experiencing them and the thoughts that go through your mind at the time. This book will help you master them all. And, if it is a loved one, friend or colleague who suffers anxiety, it can also help you to help them.

Very often, when we come to understand something, the fear is taken out of it. So, in Part 1, 'Understanding anxiety', we explain exactly what is going on in our bodies when anxiety overwhelms us, and why it happens. This should give you the confidence to go on and tackle the thoughts and feelings that exacerbate anxiety's effects. We show you exactly how to do this in Part 2, 'Overcoming anxiety', with practical ways to manage your thoughts and feelings to change your experience for the better.

Many of the steps you can take to help yourself are applicable, whatever form your anxiety takes. However, we also look at and explain individual anxiety disorders and give specific advice on each. For example, for certain often very distressing types of anxiety, there is a safe, swift treatment available that can neutralise the emotionally arousing images that produce seemingly irrational fears – this then frees you to react more appropriately to non-threatening objects and events. We explain this in detail, along with other examples of effective counselling for anxiety, in Part 3, 'Seeking professional help'.

As we have mentioned, anxiety is a natural survival mechanism. But if it gets out of control, it means something isn't working properly in our lives. This could be because one or more of our essential needs aren't being met well, or in balance, or because the innate resources which were designed to help us meet our needs (such as our imagination) aren't functioning as they should, for any of a variety of reasons. Because these innate needs and resources are built into our biology, we call them the human 'givens'. As you will discover, identifying and addressing missing needs and learning to make the best use of our

> 66 Many of the steps you can take are applicable whatever form your anxiety takes ... 99

resources – our natural guidance system – are at the heart of the human givens approach (which underpins the information offered in this book). But this doesn't mean endlessly poking around in the past, looking for hidden causes or complicated explanations: it simply means mastering effective ways to ensure yourself a better future.

Taking some time to read and absorb the information and skills presented in this book will serve you well for the rest of your life.

PLEASE NOTE: To protect confidentiality, the biographical details in the case histories used in this book have been changed.

PART 1

Understanding anxiety

NXIETY can take many forms. Maybe, when you wake in the morning and open your eyes, a vague, unidentifiable feeling of fear or anxiety envelops you. You are aware of your heart beating quickly, or even banging in your chest. Or perhaps you feel just a fluttering sensation. You may have to concentrate to breathe. You scan the room, looking for the source, but know it isn't there. The familiar sense of foreboding grows. You get out of bed and the anxiety gets out with you. Perhaps it takes the form of a churning in your stomach; or a tingling in every limb; or a suffocating fear wrapped around your throat. You tell yourself there is nothing to worry about, and might even have found ways to push the feeling away, to keep it at bay for a while, as you get on with your day. But inside you still lurks the dreadful feeling that the fear will come back again, suddenly, out of the blue, catching you unawares.

Or perhaps it comes right along with you, that unidentifiable sense of impending disaster. Your limbs are restless; your mouth is dry; your mind is racing with thoughts that you can't even catch – they slip in and out of mind so fast. Thinking clearly or concentrating on your work or daily tasks is almost impossible. And, worst of all, you have no idea why this is happening.

Or maybe your anxiety is less intrusive than that. You look perfectly normal, behave perfectly normally, get on with your life apparently normally. And yet you don't feel fulfilled or truly happy or fully in the heart of things. A lot of the time you feel panicky or nervous. You can't relax or settle down to things. "What if?" and "shouldn't I?" questions run through your mind most of the time (although you might not be aware of this yet), along with concerns about what others think of you, whether what you do is good enough, and is it worth bothering anyway, considering the state of the world? Or perhaps sometimes your mind just goes a complete blank. It might be that you are so convinced that you must do things perfectly that you often fail to complete them, or even start them, at all. The disabling anxiety is almost always there, on your shoulder, weighing you down. At night, it stops you getting off to sleep and, if you wake in the early hours, it kicks in at once, preventing you from dropping back to sleep again quickly. Sometimes, it may all be too much and you find yourself panicking.

Or else you might be going about your normal business

when, suddenly, for no reason you can fathom, your heart starts to pound; you are sweating and shaking; struggling to take in enough breath, you feel that you are choking; your stomach drops to the ground and you have the terrible feeling that you are going to lose control of your bladder and your bowels. You may feel dizzy and faint and as if you are outside of yourself. It feels as if you are going to die. All you know is that you have got to get out of wherever you are fast The doctor has told you that nothing is physically wrong with you. But that doesn't help. It is just as terrifying the next time it happens, and the next time, and the more hopeless and helpless and fearful you come to feel.

Perhaps you know why it happened the first time: maybe you started feeling nauseated and clammy and panicky on a bus because you had what turned out to be a stomach bug (although you didn't know it at the time). Yet, seemingly inexplicably, the panic now happens *every* time you get on a bus, even though you know that you are perfectly well and try your hardest to stop it. Maybe there are other times, too, when you know that you are likely to feel overwhelmingly panicked – in crowded shops or enclosed cinemas or at the sight of a dog or a bird or even broken glass. It doesn't make sense, even to you, that you should experience such terror in such circumstances, but that doesn't stop it happening. Gradually, you start to avoid places where there might be crowds or

> **"** You already have all the tools you need to take back control. **"**

birds or whatever you fear, and your life shrinks further and further. You stop doing many of the things you used to enjoy. Perhaps you are even afraid to leave the house.

Or maybe you have no idea at all what triggers the distress, and that makes you feel even more out of control.

It might be that a sudden, terrible thought starts it all off, an overwhelming fear that a loved one will die or that you might inadvertently, or even intentionally, do harm to another person or that you will be contaminated by germs. Although you spend much of the day trying to force the unwanted thoughts out of your mind, the anxiety still mounts. Perhaps you have devised ritual activities of some kind which are intended to counter the power of such thoughts: if you carry them out religiously, the event you fear won't happen and the anxiety will stop. But it never works. The thought and the anxiety come back, and so the ritual must be repeated and repeated and repeated, taking over more and more of your day. Perhaps you are good at keeping this burden a secret; or perhaps your family and friends and colleagues have started to notice that something is amiss ...

It could be that your anxiety started after being involved in or seeing – or even just being told about – a horrific life-threatening event. Distressing images and thoughts connected with the event keep flooding into mind. You might even feel as if you are continually reliving the event or you wake from nightmares that seem connected with it. You don't feel like yourself anymore; instead, you are always on the alert, fearfully watching, never relaxed, distant with people you love. You can't properly engage with life any longer, and often feel angry and irritable.

Maybe you have developed a 'nervous stomach', suffer a lot of headaches, or have found that a condition you already have, such as psoriasis or eczema, worsens. Perhaps you fidget a lot, or pull your hair or bite the inside of your lips.

There are very many different ways that severe anxiety can affect people, but there is one that is common to all. Like a tyrant, it has come to rule your life.

But that tyranny is now about to end, because this book will help put *you* back in charge. You have all the tools you need, within yourself, to take back control. Instead of anxiety working against you, crippling and choking you, it can be tamed to work *for* you, just as it was always meant to.

The first important thing to remember is this. The internal mechanism that drives your anxiety was serving you well

> 66 Instead of anxiety working against you ... it can be tamed to work *for* you, just as it was always meant to. 99

when it first went on full alert, whatever the original cause (and it really doesn't matter if you have forgotten what that was). It was doing its job – trying to keep you safe. But it is still in overdrive, even though the job has been done, and so is now doing more harm than good – just as it would do more harm than good to continue taking antibiotics for life for a throat infection that would have cleared up after one course. Why your anxiety mechanism is in overdrive and how you can bring it down to normal, effective levels are what you will learn from this book.

We can never eliminate fluctuating anxiety levels and wouldn't want to, as they have a job to do. But we do need to learn to manage them, so that anxiety can function in the way it is intended – to our benefit.

Anxiety and stress are closely linked

To understand anxiety, we need to understand about stress, because anxiety and stress are closely connected, though in two different ways. The first, perhaps most obvious, connection, is that very many anxiety problems arise because of chronic levels of stress. The second we will look at shortly.

What is stress?

Stress is any pressure or accumulation of pressures – physical or psychological – that is too much for a person to cope with comfortably. Therefore, what is perceived as a stress will vary from individual to individual. A marathon runner, for example, will have no difficulty running three miles, yet that might well tax most of the rest of us beyond our endurance. A stand-up comic may thrive on the 'rush' of performing live in front of an audience of hecklers, whereas just giving a short presentation to supportive colleagues will induce extreme panic in someone else.

Throughout our lives we may well have to cope with many highly stressful events, ranging from the death of a loved one, relationship breakdown, divorce, job loss, financial difficulties, sex problems and chronic illness to even much longed-for events such as pregnancy, a new child in the family and retirement. And less marked changes in our circumstances, such as a change of job/college/school, a deteriorating relationship with a partner or friend, grown-up child leaving home, more or less responsibility at work or difficulties with a new boss, can all take their toll.

When several events like these happen at the same time or within a short time span, we can be pushed completely beyond our normal coping capabilities. But even lots of small stressful events (or 'hassles') that mount up over the day can have a strong negative effect on us.

It is often said that stress can be good as well as bad – getting married, for instance, or setting off on holiday are eagerly anticipated activities, yet they can also be highly stressful. There is an important distinction, however, between being *stretched* and being *stressed*. When we are undertaking new challenges, whether planning a big event or learning a new skill, we *are* initially stretched beyond our comfort zone but, if we can rise to the challenge, it feels good. We feel excited. Whereas when we are stressed, we can't rise to the challenge: we feel defeated

> 66 There is an important distinction between being *stretched* and being *stressed* ... 99

and negative and that the effort is too much. It feels bad, and we feel anxious. The physiological effects are initially the same (as we will show in a moment) but the outcome very different. In the first scenario, energy is discharged and some-

The widespread rise of stress

IN OUR busy, modern lives, stress is hugely on the increase. Recent government statistics, for example, revealed that work-related stress accounts for over a third of all new episodes of ill health. And each case of stress-related ill health leads to an average of 30.9 working days lost; in 2004/5, a total of 12.8 million working days were lost to stress, depression and anxiety.[1] Indeed, sickness absence surveys have consistently shown that 30–35 per cent of employee sick leave in the UK is related to these same three factors.[2] The insurance company UnumProvident has calculated that, between 1995 and 2001, changes in work patterns in the UK resulted in a 50 per cent increase in claims for compensation arising from mental and psychological problems.[3] Another insurance company, Norwich Union, reports on their website that one in every three claims is for mental illness, including stress, and this number has risen steadily over the last ten years.

In short, severe anxiety and fear-related disorders are a major and widespread problem that, surveys show, affect up to 18 per cent of the UK population. The Human Givens Institute's emotional needs audit of a large sample of the population confirms this, with 24 per cent self-reporting that they feel insecure in at least one major area of their life. (Visit: www.enaproject.org for further details.)

1. Department of Health (1995), *ABC of Health Promotion in the Workplace: A Resource Pack for Employees*. London: Department of Health.
2. CBI (1995), *Managing Absence*. CBI/Centre File Survey. London: CBI.
3. UnumProvident (2002), *The Living Insurer*. See: www.unumprovident.co.uk

thing is achieved; in the second, there is nothing to show for it. This is an important difference that needs to be more widely understood.

In human givens terms, which we will be explaining fully later, all forms of stress arise because, in one way or another (for whatever reason), one or more essential physical or emotional needs are not being met in a person's life. It may be something that happens gradually – starting, perhaps, with loneliness due to the loss of a loved partner or the inability, because of overwhelming shyness, to make new friends – and then builds and builds in an insidious way, taking the light and enjoyment out of life. Or it may be something that happens suddenly, as on those tragic occasions when people, whose lives were working well, are caught up in a natural disaster or become the victims of violence – everything is changed in a flash, and their lives become ruled by fear, making it harder and harder for them to get their essential needs met.

When all of our needs are being met in balance and we are confident about our place in the world and about how we go about in it, we *don't* suffer from seriously disabling anxiety and stress.

How do we know if we are under stress?

If we are struggling to cope with day-to-day living, this can manifest itself in a variety of ways, such as:

■ disturbed sleep

■ physical complaints – certain conditions, such as asthma, angina, heart disease, migraine, skin complaints, high blood pressure, irritable bowel, peptic ulcer, rheumatoid arthritis and some cancers, can be triggered or exacerbated by stress

■ excessive alcohol consumption or the taking of drugs

■ depression

■ burnout – this particularly affects dedicated professionals such as doctors, teachers and social workers who become overly involved in their work, and so don't keep their lives in balance

■ anxiety disorders.

We all have different ways of expressing the excess demands on our body systems that we experience when we are under extreme pressure, and anxiety disorders are just one of them. *Suffering extreme anxiety is not a sign of weakness or lack of moral fibre: it is purely a response to stress.*

Ongoing stress causes serious wear and tear on the body, whereas, if something stressful suddenly happens during the day and we take action to deal with it, the stress dissipates. In fact, we can even feel a sense of achievement when we've dealt with it. This is because 'dealing with it' is exactly what our bodies were designed to do. Way back in our evolutionary past, when predators were a daily source of danger, anything that could be perceived as a threat to our safety had to be responded to at once, in order to ensure our survival. We still have that survival mechanism now: it is known as the 'fight-or-flight response'. And it is the other reason that anxiety and stress are so interlinked. For, physiologically, anger, fear and anxiety are very close cousins, and they are all natural reactions to stress-inducing threats.

The fight-or-flight response

Imagine for a moment that we are our long-ago ancestors, still living in the wild. Our very survival depends on our being ready to react instantly, if a wild boar thunders out of the undergrowth or members of a hostile tribe come over the hill towards us. As soon as we sense a threat, a cascade of bodily events is triggered to help us cope. Almost instantly, the following happens:

Our muscles tense ready for action. Our blood pressure goes up, to increase the circulation to our muscles and heart, which beats faster, to cope with the expected increased demands on it. We breathe faster, to speed up the time oxygen takes to get into our blood, and that makes our chests hurt and our bodies tremble. To divert as much blood as possible to our limbs to aid action, our digestion is interrupted, making our saliva dry up, and our kidney, intestine and bladder functions stop, causing the muscles at the opening of the anus and bladder to start to relax. We sweat, to try to cool ourselves. Our bodies are flooded with 'stress' hormones that enable all these responses to happen and, as a result, we immediately flee the wild boar or fight the unwelcome tribesmen.

Once the threat is over, if we are still alive to tell the tale that is, our hearts slowly pound less, the shaking gradually stops and the sick feeling passes, as our blood circulation returns to normal and digestion and the other regulatory functions start up again. The stress hormones that were swarming through our body have been burned up during the action we took or else are neutralised as our body maintenance gets back to usual business.

This excellent system has served us well for millions of years. But it was designed to deal with circumstances in which we could take action. The stresses we face today are less often of the life-threatening kind. More usually, we find ourselves in circumstances where we feel psychologically threatened (the boss is critical of our work; someone else is getting our promotion; we're being bullied at college; a neighbour is continually picking arguments). Or we feel unsafe (we may fear walking the streets at night or meeting gangs of teenagers; the news is full of gloomy predictions about wars and global warming and deadly diseases). Or we feel 'cornered' – but not by a wild beast that we can flee – we are stuck in a traffic jam; work deadlines are unrealistic; the phone keeps ringing.

The very primitive, early-developed part of our brain (which gives the directions that set our fight-or-flight response in motion) is not able to distinguish between events like those above which it *perceives* as threatening and those that actually *are* life threatening. Even worse, it cannot distinguish between real or imagined life-threatening events either. ("I'll die if I have to get up on that stage and speak!") Indeed, when the fight-or-flight mechanism first evolved, we didn't have a 'thinking' brain and there was no such thing as imagination. So now, if we imagine ourselves experiencing disaster vividly enough, we can still easily trigger off the fight-or-flight response.

> " The very primitive part of our brain ... can't distinguish between real or imagined life-threatening events. "

But, when we are being criticised by the boss, sitting stewing in a traffic jam or imagining being trapped in a lift, there is nowhere to run to and no one to fight. And, although the physiological arousal that is switched on when we get stressed in such ways is mopped up quite quickly, an expectation – that something will or should happen – also gets switched on in the brain, and stays switched on, taking up our attention and

> 66 Taking appropriate action of some kind both relieves the stress and helps us avoid developing anxiety. 99

energy. This is a cumulative process and, with each additional stress, not only does more and more arousal occur but more and more expectation patterns stay switched on in our brains. Eventually this puts too much stress on us physically and it is at this point that one person might start to develop headaches or angina; another will turn to drink; and *you* may develop an anxiety disorder. Whatever the reaction, it is the body's message that it has been pushed too far.

Of course, stressful events will always happen. Some will drop out of the blue to scupper our plans, however well we may think we have prepared for every eventuality. At some point, someone we love will die. Companies go bust. Fires, floods and other natural disasters are all out of our control. But what *is* within our control is learning how to *deal* with stress when it arises. By taking appropriate action of some kind, we can dissipate the stress hormones – this both relieves the stress and helps us to avoid developing anxiety. (We will look in detail at how to do this in Part 2.) So, while we can't prevent a lot of the stressful events we face in life, we *can* develop psychological robustness.

Anxiety is usually what you make it

As you may well have experienced yourself, the symptoms of anxiety are not hard and fast. They can be any or all of those already described as part of the fight-or-flight response. The more severe the anxiety, the more numerous the symptoms may be. But different people may be particularly aware of some symptoms rather than others – for instance, sweating hands, quick breathing, a plummeting feeling in the stomach. Some people may have a 'racy' feeling throughout their body or a strong desire to urinate or have a bowel movement. What defines the feelings as anxiety, however, is a sense of dread or fear.

But, wait a minute. Imagine yourself as young and single. Maybe you *are* young and single. Or maybe you have to dig back into your memory a bit. Whichever it is, cast your mind

Warning!

IN A small number of cases, anxiety symptoms can be triggered by a physical condition, such as heart and lung irregularities, an undiagnosed thyroid disorder, inner ear disturbance and epilepsy. Drinking coffee or other drinks containing caffeine can make some people edgy and anxious. Equally, suddenly cutting out caffeine can have the same effect. So can suddenly stopping drinking alcohol or suddenly stopping taking tranquillisers.

back for a moment – what was it like when you first set eyes on someone you were attracted to who was also clearly attracted to you? And how did it feel when you

> **How we interpret our bodily sensations is a large part of how we experience them and record them in our memory.**

waited to go on your first date with someone you were extremely keen on? Did your heart thump a bit faster? Did you have mild palpitations? Were there butterflies in your stomach? Or did your hands feel annoyingly clammy? Yet those were good feelings – ones we associate with excitement or pleasant expectation.

These are the kinds of feelings we have whenever we are about to experience something we find enjoyably emotionally arousing: for some people, that might include hurtling down a water slide; for others, it could be singing a solo in the dramatic society's play or taking a penalty kick. If we don't enjoy those particular activities, however, the physical sensations will be the same, *but*, because they are accompanied by fear or dread, we will experience them as anxiety.

How we interpret our bodily sensations is, therefore, a large part of how we experience them and record them in our memory. An ingenious experiment, in which young men were asked to cross a long, narrow suspension bridge made of wooden boards and wire cables that rocked and swayed 230 feet above the Capilano River in North Vancouver clearly demonstrated this. A young woman researcher approached each of the men in turn to ask if they would mind completing a survey and, after they had done so, she gave them her telephone number and offered to explain the project in greater detail, if they called. She approached some of the men while they were crossing and others after they had crossed. It was found that the men she approached while they were crossing the bridge were more likely to call her. Why? Because they were experiencing physiological arousal that they would normally have identified as fear. But, because they were being interviewed by an attractive woman, they mistakenly identified their arousal as sexual attraction.

So, unless we are talking about a truly terrifying situation, in which our fight-or-flight response automatically operates at full throttle, we do have some degree of choice about how we interpret or react to fight-or-flight symptoms. A daunting activity, such as giving a talk or taking an exam or perhaps entering a party, can be less paralysing and anxiety inducing if we treat it as a challenge instead of a threat. For the whole point of the fight-or-flight system is to get us ready to *do* something and, by doing it, we disperse the anxiety. Most of us are probably familiar with the feeling of relief, or even euphoria, that may

> 66 The whole point of the fight-or-flight system is to get us ready to <u>do</u> something. 99

surface after we have successfully achieved something that we were really nervous of attempting.

At this point you may well be thinking, 'if only it *were* that easy to change how we think!' Because it isn't always, is it? However, there is a very good physiological reason for this: our emotions come first. Once we understand what is going on – that we react emotionally, before we think – we *can* start to master it, and changing how we think becomes much, much easier.

The powerful emotional brain

The 'thinking' part of our brains (the neocortex) is relatively new in evolutionary terms. Before our brains developed into the awesome organs they are now, enabling us to plan, imagine, analyse things and make judgements, we relied for our survival on our more primitive 'mammalian' brain. The mammalian brain, a set of structures which lie underneath the neocortex, is often termed the 'emotional brain', because it is concerned with instinctive responses involving emotions – most notably the fight-or-flight (anger or fear) response. All instinctive behaviour concerns survival: feeding, mating, fighting or fleeing. And our instincts induce emotions that require us to take action (ideally to carry out the instinctive behaviour so as to lower the arousal again). All emotional needs (see, 'The human givens', on page 93) arise out of this fundamental survival programme.

When the neocortex developed, we had rational intelligence at our disposal, as well as emotional intelligence, and, in the ordinary everyday, the two intelligences work together in partnership, with the rational brain adding subtlety and perspective to the raw feelings of the emotional brain, and the emotional brain tempering the rational brain's cool clinical judgements. But emotions can often overpower the rational brain, as we shall see.

The emotional brain contains a very small and powerful structure known as the amygdala – so called because it is almond-shaped and amygdala in ancient Greek means almond. In effect, the amygdala acts as the body's alarm system. It has access to our store of emotional memories and learned responses and its job is to be alert to any possible danger to us by matching new events to patterns in its store and, from that, judging whether we might be at risk. For instance, suppose we are walking alone down a dark street late at night and there is a sudden unexpected crunching sound or a quick movement. Our attention is drawn to it instantly and, in less than a split second, our amygdala decides whether the sound or movement could signify danger. It pattern matches the sound to the crunch of footsteps. It pattern matches the movement to that of a person darting out of an alleyway. Making its best guess, on the basis of what it knows from its memory stores that the sound or movement could signify, the amygdala takes the worst-case scenario and sets off the alarm. In effect, it concludes, "We are under threat! Or, at least, we might be! So we had better be ready to turn and fight or else run for it."

Because it needs to make an instant decision to get us out of any potential danger as quickly as possible, the amygdala's pattern matching is very crude. It is black and white – a situation is either safe or it isn't. Therefore, it doesn't have the sophistication of the thinking brain, which can introduce some shades of grey to the situation and might conclude that, yes, the crunch is definitely footsteps but the owner of the feet, far from being a psychopathic killer, is probably only a neighbour from down the street. And the sense of movement from the alleyway is not a shadowy alien figure with ill intent but merely a black bin bag blowing in the breeze.

> 66 Strong emotions focus and lock our attention ... everything is simplified to a black-or-white choice ... 99

But, at this point, the thinking brain hasn't yet had a look in. When the amygdala decides that we might be under threat, it takes the steps required (by sending chemical signals) to set the fight-or-flight response in motion without seeking any by your leave from the neocortex. In fact, this has all already happened by the time the neocortex gets to know what is going on half a second later. Our heart is already pounding, our legs shaking and our breathing coming short and quick by the time we recognise Bob or Nancy from two doors down or identify the bin bag. We quickly calm down then, of course, and become reasonable people again, instead of gibbering wrecks.

Emotional arousal makes us stupid

If you are going to learn to handle anxiety, this is crucial to understand: when the amygdala is centre stage, excitedly setting off alarms like this to save our skins, it is so powerful that it can actually shut down our higher intelligence completely. It is as if it has a simple on/off button that it can use to deactivate the thinking part of our brains. When our bodies are in a state of high emotional arousal (whether we are angry, terrified or head over heels in love), *we are not thinking straight*. High emotional arousal makes us temporarily stupid. Or, to put it more politely, it reduces our options to a simple choice to force us to take action.

It has to be this way. For example, if from down the street you see a motorbike up on the pavement, accelerating towards you, you don't want your thinking brain weighing up the odds and wondering, "Surely he knows he shouldn't be on the pavement? Maybe it's a film stunt? In that case, where are the cameras? Is that a Harley-Davidson he's riding? Hmmm ... actually he is going *very* fast. And he is driving straight at me! I wonder if I should just step out of the way in case he hasn't seen me...?" By that time, you might well be dead. So, in such life-or-death circumstances, we don't want a highly intelligent system that can carry out reasoned analysis. We want an excitable (and therefore stupid) system that can terrify us and make us dodge the bike and run for it before we even know what we are doing!

So sometimes panic is the right response. In other circumstances, however, the 'threat' might turn out to be harmless and, if you have already legged it, you might well feel a prize fool. But your amygdala doesn't care whether you get embarrassed or not. It knows that you can get embarrassed a hundred times and it won't kill you; but fail to act on a genuine life-or-death threat just once, and you are likely to end up never needing this wonderful survival mechanism again.

The dimmer switch

Of course, as we've already acknowledged, most of the threats we face today are *not* of the life-or-death variety. But we still need the fight-or-flight response to stay intact for those occasions when calamity really could strike – to help us avoid the speeding car, falling tree or flying missile, for example, or deal with any other emergency.

There is a problem with the system, though. If it's activated in less than life-or-death circumstances and the fear feelings which are aroused aren't acted upon in any way, the emotional arousal will continue – which means we won't be thinking at our best. So, not only is the amygdala able to make us take actions *before* the neocortex even knows anything about it; it can also keep the neocortex functioning under par for long periods of time. In other words, as well as having an on/off switch for the neocortex; it operates a dimmer switch too. If we remain partially emotionally aroused, then we are partially stupid – or, dimmer!

This is what will have happened if you have ever revised really hard for an exam, yet, once you were in the examination room, your mind went completely blank and suddenly all that hard-learned material was totally unavailable to you. If you had previously been imagining taking the exam and worrying about not doing well, your amygdala is quite likely to have made the pattern match that being in the exam room constituted a threat. Consequently, it sets up a low-grade fight-or-flight response, and your anxiety denies you full access to your thinking brain; anxiety has thus caused many an intelligent mind to go blank whilst taking exams. As we've mentioned, the amygdala's pattern matching is a crude

> 66 Your anxiety denies you full access to your thinking brain. 99

process. It looks for broad similarities, not distinctive details. Thus it can't tell the difference between an event that we have been worrying about in our imagination and one that has really happened. It sets off the alarm bells, regardless.

Memories are not set in stone

And there is another big problem. Once that disastrous exam situation has occurred for real, rather than just being a worry, the amygdala is able to confirm it as a definite a threat to our wellbeing and is all the more ready to raise the alarm, should it occur again. Therefore, how we approached having to take the exam, and how we interpreted our 'exam nerves', will have affected the way in which we recorded the experience of exam taking in our memory. But, fortunately, memories are not set in stone. If our experience becomes different, we can change the memories, so that they cease to come up as a pattern match with apparently life-threatening circumstances. (If a memory is traumatic, however, and thus deeply etched, a skilled therapist can use a simple procedure, known as the 'rewind technique', to achieve this effect. It takes the emotion out of the memory, thus lowering the associated arousal and freeing up the thinking brain. We describe it in Part 3.)

So, as we have seen, when the amygdala is in full flow, it is sending a cascade of signals to the neocortex, inhibiting its ability to understand and analyse situations, and forcing us into emotional black-and-white, all-or-nothing thinking that prevents us from being able to consider other possibilities and take a wider viewpoint. The ultimate black-and-white thought is, of course, "Shall I fight or shall I flee?" (Indeed, some people do flee from exam rooms.) But there are many other varieties of black-and-white thinking that strongly serve to increase anxiety and keep it going. We are going to look at these next.

Black-and-white thinking

You might be interested to identify whether you have a tendency towards emotional black-and-white thinking – that is, on the basis of rather limited evidence, taking a viewpoint that excludes wider possibilities or greater options. Below are some common examples, take a moment to read them through. Do you ever have any thoughts like these?

■ *All-encompassing*

Making a broad assumption based on one, possibly trivial, fact.

"Alison is a better person than I am: she makes better cakes/ has a higher degree/ is always smiling."

"Anyone who thinks that must be an idiot."

"If something can go wrong, it will."

"Eating Chinese food is risky. It made me sick once."

■ *Self-focusing*

Believing there must be a personal significance behind what are actually random events.

> *"That's the third time this week the bus to work has been too crowded for me to get on. I must have done something bad to deserve this."*

> *"The computer doesn't like me. It keeps going on the blink."*

■ *Jumping to conclusions*

Reaching a judgement on the basis of one, often insignificant, fact or event.

> *"My husband/wife is late home. He/she is having an affair!"*

> *"When I came in to work this morning, the sales director was talking to Sarah. He's going to give her the promotion!"*

> *"My neighbour's milk is still on the step. He must be dead in his bed!"*

> *"My mother suffered from anxiety. So I'll always suffer from anxiety too."*

■ *Blaming*

The tendency to look for someone or something specific to carry the can when things go wrong – very often oneself.

> *"It's all my fault that my husband/wife/boyfriend/girlfriend has left me."*

"Trust me to go and work for a company that went bust six months later."

"I think parents are to blame if their children turn out badly."

"I put it all down to the weather."

■ *Exaggerating feelings*

Sensations and emotions are misconstrued as much more negatively meaningful than they really are.

Feeling a bit sad:
  "I must be depressed!" "I might as well kill myself."

Anxiety makes the heart thump a bit:
  "Am I having a heart attack?"

Feeling a little nervous:
  "I can't cope!"

Having a nasty headache:
  "I might have a brain tumour!"

■ *Taking a position*

Being unable to countenance that someone else might have a different but equally valid viewpoint or that there is a middle way.

  "Helping a terminally ill person to die is always wrong" /
  "Helping a terminally ill person to die is always right".

"You are either a winner or a loser."

"If you aren't part of the solution, you are part of the problem."

"If you don't do it to the best of your ability, it isn't worth doing it at all."

■ Catastrophising

Assuming the outcome of an event is going to be personally disastrous.

"If I mess this up, I'll never get another chance!"

"If I don't get this report in by tomorrow, my boss will kill me!"

"I can't start the car. I'll lose my job if I'm late!"

"If he/she dumps me, my whole life will be ruined!"

■ Having to be perfect

Imposing impossible or restricting demands on oneself.

"You can't be seen out not looking your best."

"My essays have got to be absolutely brilliant before I'll give them in. Trouble is, I keep missing the deadlines."

"I got graded 'excellent' seven times and 'good' once. Oh dear, why did I only get 'good'?"

"I'll have nothing but the best for my children. I'd rather they went without than made do."

■ *Obfuscating*

Jumping on convoluted, psychological explanations for events that might be more simply explained in a different way.

"You don't like me because you've got a thing about men/women."

"I failed because I have a fear of success."

"You continually put down my efforts because you have an unconscious need to sabotage whatever I do."

■ *Putting oneself down*

"I only won the competition because no one really good entered."

"I can't blame anyone for not picking me. Why should they?"

"Anything I do is likely to turn out badly."

The three pertinent Ps

The ways in which we explain the negative events that happen to us and to others in the world have a considerable bearing on whether we are likely to suffer from excessive anxiety. As you can probably now see, the types of thinking just described are limiting rather than empowering. Three particular types of limiting thinking (of which there are examples above) are especially connected with the development of anxiety and its close partner, depression. We call them the three Ps, they are:

- how *personally* you take events
- how *pervasive* you think the effects will be
- how *permanent* you think the effects will be.

You might like to see for yourself whether you have a tendency towards any of them, by thinking about the following scenarios.

EXERCISE:

How personally do you take events?

- If you were passed over for promotion, would you assume it was your fault for not being good enough? Would you beat yourself up about it? (Or would you consider other factors, such as the successful candidate's superior qualifications or greater experience or even the role of politicking in the decision?)

- If a friend doesn't ring you when she said she was going to, to arrange a cinema visit, do you agonise about what you might have done to offend her? Might you assume you can't be important enough for her to bother about? Or that it isn't surprising that she hasn't rung because she has probably found someone better to go with? (Or might you think that something unexpected has probably cropped up that she has had to deal with? Or that it has quite simply slipped her mind and that she'll remember later?)

- If a family holiday doesn't work out as well as you hoped, is it your fault for some reason? Perhaps you didn't research the destination well enough? Or you didn't organise enough activities to interest your partner and the children? Or perhaps you weren't sensitive enough to everyone's needs? Do you worry about it afterwards? (Or might you think that neither your partner nor the children took enough responsibility for making sure they had fun? That the resort was not quite the paradise the brochure made it out to be? That it was a shame someone or other in your party developed a really bad cold and so felt pretty miserable thereafter?)

How pervasive do you think the effects will be?

- If you were to lose your job, would you think your whole life was in crisis and that nothing could go right for you? Would losing your job take the colour completely out of everything you usually enjoy, such as hobbies or time spent with the family? Would you be difficult to be around? Would you withdraw from people and become absorbed in catastrophic thinking? (Or would you be shocked and upset but make sure that you drew comfort from everything that is working well in your life, such as family relationships and friendships, and think practically about what to do next?)

- If your relationship with a spouse or partner ended, might you become uninterested in the job that you normally enjoy? Would you have no interest in seeing friends or pay less attention than usual to your children's needs? Would you think your whole life was ruined and worry about what will become of you? (Or would you be devastated but grateful for the many resources, such as your job and your relationship with your friends and/or children, that you can call on to help you through this difficult time?)

- If you were to suffer a physical loss such as a limb or your sight or to develop a chronic, disabling illness, would you consider your life might as well be over and that you could never feel happy and fulfilled again? Would you dwell on all the things you that you couldn't ever again do and be convinced you couldn't even start to cope? (Or would you grieve for the loss but then move on to find ways to make the most of the abilities you have?)

How permanent do you think the effects will be?

- If you have, in the past, experienced the break up of a much-valued relationship, did you think for some time that you would never have another one? Or at least never have another one with someone you cared about so much? If a current relationship ended, would you think it irreplaceable ever? (Or would you grieve and then gradually become open to finding someone new?)

- If you were to lose your job, would you worry that you would never find another that fit your particular skill set so well? (Or would you set about maximising your chances for getting an even better one, or take the opportunity to explore some completely different possibilities?)

- If you did less than brilliantly in the one exam you needed to pass especially well, in order to study for a chosen profession, would you think that you had ruined your chances forever? (Or would you brush up on your weak areas and retake the exam? Or decide that you might be better suited to a different career, and explore other options?)

Clearly, if you have answered 'yes' more often to the questions that aren't inside the brackets, you have a tendency towards anxious (and depressive) thinking. It might be worth considering the typical anxieties that bother you and checking whether you are indeed viewing them as personal, pervasive and/or permanent.

> ** Anxious thoughts help keep the emotional arousal going. **

Not only are anxious thoughts of the kinds discussed above the products of black-and-white emotional thinking; they actually help keep the emotional arousal, and therefore the anxiety, going. This is because the thoughts themselves generate more and more emotion. Of course you feel anxious if you believe that, if something isn't perfect, it is a complete disaster! But most of the time, things *aren't* perfect. And of course you feel anxious if you think the bad times are never going to end or that all aspects of life will become problematic as a result of a single setback.

Anxiety is usually a misuse of the imagination

This brings us on to another major cause of anxiety – whatever form it takes: our imagination. Anxious people tend to have very good imaginations, the trouble is they continually, albeit unintentionally, misuse them to generate emotionally arousing worry.

For example, if you are always lying awake in the wee

hours, worrying "What if?" and imagining ever more dire outcomes for yourself or those you care about, you are generating vivid, negative fantasies that keep you in a constant state of fight-or-flight arousal. If you are fearful of spiders or cats or bird feathers or mirrors or metals, you may spend a lot of your time imagining scenarios in which you might come across them, as well as imagining the panic you will feel. If you carry out compulsive rituals to ward off bad things from happening, you may also spend a lot of time imagining the bad outcomes that the rituals are intended, however vainly, to prevent. And so forth.

> " ... generating vivid, negative fantasties keeps you in a constant state of fight-or-flight arousal. "

Imagination is not innocuous. It is a powerful, useful tool, but it can also undermine some people, particularly those prone to pessimism. In Part 2 we will discover how to turn that power to good.

Now that it should be clear what is going on physiologically, mentally and emotionally when we are over-anxious, we can better understand what is happening in particular types of anxiety disorders. Let's take a look at them one by one, in the light of these new understandings.

UNDERSTANDING ANXIETY | 37

Generalised anxiety

Generalised anxiety is extremely common. Doctors diagnose
what they term 'generalised anxiety disorder' if someone has
been worrying for a minimum of six months about at least
two specific stressful life events – an impending divorce,
redundancy, bereavement or financial problems, for instance
– and has been experiencing a range of anxiety symptoms,
such as:

- feeling agitated
- irritability
- inability to relax
- difficulty concentrating
- mind going blank
- feelings of foreboding
- continual worrying
- feelings of depression

and accompanying physical symptoms of anxiety, such as

- muscle tension
- difficulty sleeping
- restlessness
- headaches
- fatigue
- upset stomach
- dry mouth

- heart palpitations
- sweatiness
- dizziness
- quick, shallow breathing.

It doesn't really matter, however, whether you meet these criteria or not. What matters is that you are suffering from a degree of anxiety that is adversely affecting your life at the moment and you want to do something about it.

People who have generalised anxiety don't suffer from panic attacks or phobias but they do feel overtaken by a sense of fear. This fear is often formless or else may be centred on something that it isn't irrational to fear (such as illness, child-birth or dying) but they feel unable to do anything to help themselves face it more calmly. Sometimes worries may focus on an inability to cope, fears of failure, children's welfare or sexual performance. Whatever the cause, the worries often become all pervading. For instance, a sense of apprehension may be triggered if a person finds that they have to take a different bus or route from the one that they usually take; or that they need to go to a part of the country they have never visited before; or to visit the dentist; or study a new course. Or they may spend time worrying about whether their children are being molested at school or their elderly mother has managed to get safely to the shops and back. One woman described her anxiety in terms of a dial. "Other people's dials are at zero, unless they have reason to turn them on. I'm never below a 1, even at my best."

It is a highly uncomfortable, troubling feeling to be anxious almost all of the time and it takes a toll on our body, of course. For now we know that the symptoms described above are either elements of the fight-or-flight response or the physical or psychological consequences of not being able to take action to dispel the arousal. The stress hormones keep on circulating and we are in a state of almost constant hyper-alert.

Generalised anxiety often starts during a period when we have to deal with more major stresses than we can cope with at any one time. These could include financial difficulties, a serious illness (our own or that of someone close to us), trouble at work or an important relationship breakdown, and even events that one might think of as being positive, such as having a baby, moving house or starting college. It can also develop after traumatic events, such as abuse or a serious accident. A client of Ivan's, for instance, developed an anxiety disorder after enduring an unexpected, dramatic and cruel humiliation at work. Some people are more prone to anxiety responses because of the kind of thinking styles we looked at earlier. Others lack confidence generally in themselves and in

> 66 There are new actions you can take and skills you can learn to help you live your life with pleasure again. 99

their abilities, and so worry more about a great many things.

Whatever the reasons, if you recognise yourself in these descriptions, there are new actions you can take and new skills you can learn that will help you live your life, with pleasure, instead of fearing it.

How poor sleep can turn worry into depression

Disturbed sleep is an extremely common feature of generalised anxiety. This is distressing and debilitating enough in itself but it also plays a significant part in the feelings of depression that often accompany anxiety, as we shall explain.

Everybody appreciates a good night's sleep. But what constitutes a good night's sleep is much more complex than previously thought. Sleep is not just the brain turning off and resting. Every night, we need a quota of two kinds – slow-wave sleep and dream sleep (also called rapid eye movement or REM sleep because our eyes dart around behind our closed eyelids during this phase). During slow-wave sleep, the day-to-day wear and tear on our bodily tissues is repaired; brain cells are recharged with sugars and our immune system is refreshed. But, in dream sleep, our brain services our emotional intelligence system. In effect, dreaming is an inbuilt super stress-control mechanism, one of nature's most incredible developments, without which complex mammals like us could not have evolved. So, to use a computer analogy, slow-wave sleep repairs the hardware and dream sleep repairs the software – our thoughts and emotions.

After 12 years of research, trying to puzzle out why we evolved to dream, one of this book's authors, Joe Griffin, showed that the role of dreaming is to deactivate the emotional expectations that we get worked up about during the day and which are still taking up space in our brains when we fall asleep.* He discovered that what needs

> **❝ Dreaming frees up our brains to face the next day's emotional concerns. ❞**

discharging are not the arousals that were *expressed* during the day, perhaps by having a heated argument with our partner, or taking evasive action, such as steering round and managing to avoid a dramatic motorway accident; it is the arousals that *aren't expressed* or acted out that produce dreams. These arousals stew away all day below consciousness, waiting to be dealt with, and, if they are still there when we fall asleep, the arousal pattern is completed by being acted out metaphorically in our dreams. This frees up our brains to face the next day's emotional concerns. In other words, we dream out the emotionally arousing expectations, which, unconsciously, our emotional brain was still expecting to have happen.

This is one of those scientific discoveries that is easy to

---

* Griffin, J. and Tyrrell, I. (2004) *Dreaming Reality: How dreaming keeps us sane, or can drive us mad.* HG Publishing, East Sussex.

confirm from your own experience. Every day we generate countless expectations – emotional arousals, positive or negative – that don't work out. These can range from major ones, such as setting one's heart on a new house but not knowing if things are going to work out, to minor ones, like considering for a moment taking a proffered piece of cake and then thinking better of it. Thoughts about the house would keep surfacing, even though we might instantly forget the cake, but both expectations would remain live in the brain at an instinctive, emotional level. This is because a primitive urge has been activated – to move towards something that is desired (the house) or to eat something (the cake) – and, just like other primitive survival urges (for sex, warmth or safety etc.), it has to be discharged in some way or another, once aroused.

This is as true for other mammals as it is for us. If the urges didn't get discharged, our survival instincts would weaken. For what would be the point of having the instincts that urge us to eat, drink, run away, have sex, etc., if we ignored them most of the time? Yet we do override them a great deal of the time because we don't eat every time we see something that whets our appetite or have sex every time we see a person that attracts us. Clearly, we still need those instincts available to us for the right times and places. So nature's clever way to keep instinctive programmes intact is to 'act out' or complete in our dreams the expectations that were not fulfilled while we were awake.

The brain can only do this when all the senses are shut down, as they are in REM sleep. And, because we can't fulfil the expectations in 'real' time, the brain uses metaphors, patterns drawn from memory, that correspond emotionally to the expectations not acted out.

The unfulfilled expectations that give rise to dreams can be surprisingly varied. For instance, even seeing something on television that makes us angry or alarmed can be sufficient to generate a dream. (As parents are well aware, children often wake up from nightmares generated by something scary seen on the telly.) More importantly, for our purposes here, an almost bottomless pit of unfulfilled expectations is produced by ... constant worrying. And that brings its own special problems.

Let us imagine that Elizabeth, instead of dropping off into a comfortable, soothing sleep when she goes to bed, lies there every night with different worries going round and round in her head – "What if I don't get the car to the garage the minute it opens. I'll have to wait in the queue to book it in and then I'll be late for the train. Then I'll have no time to get the room prepared for the meeting. And what if I don't get a seat on the train? I can't stand with my bad back. But it would be so embarrassing to ask for a seat! Lucy's got her mock maths GCSE tomorrow. I wonder if she packed her calculator. I'm sure I saw it downstairs, when she was studying. Did she pick it up? I think she must have. Or did she? I must remember to check the table when I get up. Perhaps I should do it now? No, it's too cold. Oh, I'd better. No, it will disturb the cat, if I go down there. He'll think I'm going to feed him ..." By thinking all this, Elizabeth is reliably building up more and more software maintenance for her poor dreaming brain to carry out. And that is added to all the worries that have been whirring around in her head all day that are already in the queue.

Dream overload

Dream (REM) sleep is a wonderful mechanism. But, just as two aspirins can be helpful in curing a headache, whereas taking the whole bottle would be harmful, so the right amount of REM sleep accomplishes the emotional repairs required but too much is counter-productive. In addition, if you give the dreaming brain too much work to do, it is forced to up the amount of REM sleep you have each night, which isn't healthy.

The normal sleep pattern is to start the night with slow-wave body-repair sleep, followed about 90 minutes later by our first period of REM sleep, which lasts about 10 minutes. As the night goes on, we gradually have less slow wave sleep and more REM sleep, culminating in about half an hour of REM sleep just before we wake up in the morning (which is why we sometimes remember the last dream we have had). As a rule, though, we usually forget our dreams, because they represent expectations that *didn't* get completed in real life and therefore we don't want them stored in memory, as if they had been.

However, research has shown that depressed people who worry a lot have their first REM sleep just 20 minutes (or at most 50) into the night, and it can last for almost an hour They then continue to have more and longer periods of REM sleep (and more intense dreams) until the brain can take no more and they wake in the early hours, even more exhausted than when they went to sleep. Then, once awake, they start all the worrying all over again.

We have an electrical signalling system in our brains – sometimes called the orientation response – that alerts us to sudden changes in our environment. (It is this that would have drawn our attention to the sound of footsteps or the darting movement in the alley that we described earlier, when discussing the amygdala's alarm system role.) This same signal is also set off at the start of and during dreaming, alerting us to the fact that there are undischarged emotional arousals which need de-arousing through dream content. Unsurprisingly, this signal goes off at an amazing rate in people who worry almost continually. Each time we respond to this signal, however, it draws on our motivational energy,

> ** Excessive REM sleep uses up our motivational energy ... **

of which we only have a certain amount. And, as excessive REM sleep pretty well uses this up, it is no surprise, then, than incessant worriers all too often wake in the morning feeling not just exhausted but depressed and lacking in the motivation to get them going.

Quite naturally, this provides something new to worry about. "Why do I feel like this? I went to bed early. And I know I had quite a bit of sleep. Why don't I feel refreshed? Why is it such a huge effort just to get out of bed and go and put the kettle on? Perhaps there's something seriously physically wrong with me?"

If this is you ...

Well, yes, something *is* physically wrong – at the moment. Your sleep pattern is out of balance, leaving you short on slow-wave body-repair sleep while your dreaming brain is in overdrive, running itself ragged trying to discharge all the arousal caused by your worrying. No wonder you don't feel good. And the longer it goes on, the greater the wear and tear on your body, as it is also under siege from all those perpetually circulating stress hormones.

Quite a dramatic scenario, isn't it? And it stems entirely from all that fretting, worrying and dread. And although your energy stores gradually fill up somewhat during the day, they quickly become depleted again when the next bout of emotional arousals comes up for discharge in dream form that night. For dreaming doesn't solve problems. It isn't intended to. It merely completes our unresolved emotional expectations so that we can start the day with a fresh 'slate', in terms of emotional arousal. By starting the worry cycle all over again, we undo all that work.

But this needn't be a permanent state of affairs. Indeed, we have found that simply knowing all this is often the spur that people need to enable them successfully to take the steps which we describe in Part 2 to stop the worrying.

Post-traumatic stress reactions

At the other extreme from the low-level continual arousal of generalised anxiety is the constant high arousal generated by post-traumatic stress. If you suffer from this it can be a truly terrifying experience.

Whenever people suddenly find themselves in a life-threatening or extremely dangerous situation, especially one in which they feel helpless, it is natural to experience intense fear and horror. This is also often our reaction if we find ourselves witnessing such an event, rather than being involved in it – or even if just a vivid portrayal or account of it has been seen or heard. Traumatic events of this kind range from surviving natural disasters, such as earthquakes, tsunamis or avalanches, to ones caused by human error, such as car, train and plane crashes, capsizing boats and sinking ships. Violent attacks such as being mugged, raped, kidnapped or sexually or physically abused, can all traumatise, as can an event such as a house fire, a complicated childbirth or suffering a heart attack. Surviving a bomb or shooting outrage, or witnessing a massacre in a war zone commonly produces post-traumatic stress symptoms. Some grandchildren of concentration camp survivors became traumatised after hearing their relatives relive their terrible memories. Imagining the terrible deaths of loved ones who didn't survive a disaster can also induce trauma, as can learning that a relative has been severely injured or that one's child is suffering a life-threatening or terminal illness.

Although it takes time to calm down and to process and cope with whatever terrifying situation has occurred, four out of five people are able to do so without lasting psychological damage.

One in five people, however, goes on to experience persistent post-traumatic stress, in which the memory of the traumatic event, instead of gradually fading or ceasing to take centre stage in their minds, keeps them helplessly and horrifyingly in thrall. The following symptoms associated with post-traumatic stress are deemed severe enough to warrant a diagnosis of post-traumatic stress disorder (PTSD).*

---

* This symptom description guide is based on the diagnostic criteria for PTSD that appear in the current edition of the American Psychiatric Association's *Diagnostic and Statistical Manual of Mental Disorders (DSM-IV)*.

The traumatic event is persistently re-experienced in one or more of the following ways:

- recurrent and intrusive distressing recollections of the event, including images, thoughts or perceptions
- recurrent distressing dreams of the event
- acting or feeling as though the event were happening all over again (a sense of re-living it, illusions, hallucinations or flashbacks, in which it feels as though the incident is being re-experienced)
- intense mental or physical distress when something internal or external triggers associations with the event – even if it is not always consciously recognised as such (for example, significant anniversaries, hearing a particular sound, the sensation of intense bodily heat).

Persistent avoidance of anything that could trigger associations with the trauma and a general numbing of feeling, manifested in three or more of the following ways:

- efforts to avoid thoughts, feelings or conversation associated with the trauma
- efforts to avoid activities, places or people that arouse recollections of the trauma
- amnesia for certain important elements of the trauma
- marked loss of interest or participation in significant activities
- feeling detached or estranged from others

- difficulty in feeling warm emotions (for instance, inability to feel loving or tender)
- sense of a blighted future (for instance, not expecting a normal career or to marry, have children or live a normal life span).

Persistent symptoms of increased arousal post-trauma, as indicated in two or more of the following ways:

- difficulty falling or staying asleep
- irritability or outbursts of anger
- difficulty in concentrating
- hypervigilance
- exaggerated startle response.

For a diagnosis of PTSD, these symptoms must have been occurring for at least a month and be causing significant distress to the person or impairment of their social life and/ or work life or other daily functioning. Looking at the list, it would be surprising if such experiences *didn't* seriously disrupt one's enjoyment of life and coping abilities. However, some people do manage to soldier on, without realising that their condition can be explained and – more importantly – very quickly resolved so their suffering can stop.

If these miserable, frightening symptoms are familiar to you and you have enough of them to cause you distress, regardless of whether they warrant an actual diagnosis of

PTSD – we urge you to seek the very swift and effective help that is available (see Part 3.)

Why some people but not others?

When people have gone through terrifying traumatic experiences, how is it that four out of five people manage to 'walk away' psychologically unharmed? There are three likely explanations.

Some life-or-death situations are more traumatising than others: If you have no means of escape from the terrifying experience, it is especially likely to become etched in your mind as a traumatic memory.

Post-traumatic stress is cumulative: The more previous traumatic situations people have found themselves in, the more likely they are to succumb at some point to PTSD. Often a police officer or a fire fighter who suffers PTSD after a particular incident comments, "But why now? Why after this? I've actually been in much worse situations before." The reason is that the stress has mounted up (becoming more than our dreaming brain can deal with) and, at the final occasion, is too much to bear. We would all eventually succumb to PTSD, if we were exposed over our lifetimes to high enough levels of traumatic stress.

How imaginative we are plays a part: After a traumatic event, it is natural for most people to 'talk' it out of their systems – for instance, talking over the details of a relative's death with different friends help us process the experience mentally and categorise it in a healthy, helpful way. But people with particularly creative temperaments or particularly vivid imaginations may imaginatively re-live and engage in the experience as they describe it to others. In effect, this is like being traumatised all over again. Remember, the amygdala (the brain organ that pattern matches to danger) doesn't know the difference between what's real and what's imagined. So reliving the trauma – whether through imaginative recall or as part of any so-called therapeutic intervention that requires a person to keep going over and re-experiencing it – makes the likelihood of suffering PTSD all the greater.

How trauma affects the brain

This brings us back neatly to the amygdala and its starring role in all this. As we explained earlier, when we are under serious threat, or we *perceive* ourselves to be under serious threat, our amygdala rushes to raise the alarm ('by setting' i.e. set the fight-or-flight response in motion) before the neocortex, the rational thinking part of our brain, even knows what is going on, let alone has a chance to form a judgement about it.

When a situation is highly traumatic, and especially if escape routes are blocked, stress levels rise *and stay* sky high.

As we have seen, high levels of emotional arousal have the effect of inhibiting any contributions from the neocortex (you can't think straight). In addition, the surge of a stress hormone known as cortisol prevents an organ in the brain called the hippocampus from being able to communicate properly with the amygdala. The hippocampus lies adjacent to the amygdala and works in partnership with it. Its normal role is to create the narrative for an event – to give it context and code it in a form that can be stored as a narrative memory in the neocortex. ("The light aircraft in which I was a passenger developed engine failure and we crashed into the trees." "When it was dark and I was walking home alone, a man in a leather jacket wrestled me to the ground, hit me and stole my wallet.") But, with the neocortex and the hippocampus virtually out of the frame, the amygdala is left to process the emotional experience all by itself, and it is too stupid to do that properly. So the traumatic situation is coded by the amygdala as a terrifying, emotionally intense feeling state – and therefore anything remotely like it must be avoided at all costs.

As we have explained, the amygdala's pattern matching abilities are crude, to say the least. So, when it has had a big fright, it makes matches all over the place. For example, if the smell of fuel was strong when the light aircraft crashed, the smell of petrol at an ordinary petrol station, while filling up the car, could be sufficient to trigger feelings of absolute terror. If a man, or even a woman, passes by in a leather jacket, panic levels may soar. Because the hippocampus has been disabled by stress, no context can be created for the terrible memory. Therefore it is, in effect, an event ever in the present, triggered by any number of sounds, sights or smells that may have only peripheral connections with the original life-threatening trauma. The inexplicable terror experienced, apparently out of the blue, makes the sufferer become hypervigilant, always tense and fearful, and increasingly unwilling to enter situations or engage in activities that might trigger such a reaction. Without context, pattern matches to a traumatic event that happened at the age of 10 can still be triggered at the age of 60, if the memory hasn't been processed properly.

Normally, within a month of a traumatic event, people's stress levels start to fall; this lets the hippocampus communicate with the amygdala again and belatedly create a context for what happened. Then, at last, the neocortex gets to have a look in. It is able to tell the panicky amygdala, "Look, I know we were in a nasty car crash. But we don't have to be frightened of getting in any car ever again. We lost control that night because the road was icy. We will certainly take better care when driving in icy conditions after this but, otherwise, we don't have anything to worry about." And, if the amygdala is calm enough to 'hear' all this, the fear of driving subsides, and things get back to normal.

But, in PTSD, because so many innocent events trigger off terror, the arousal level doesn't ever get down low enough for the hippocampus to create a context and for the neocortex to get a decent conversation going with the amygdala. It's as if the neocortex says, "But that's only petrol" or "That's only a man in a leather jacket" or "That's only a car" but the amygdala kicks and bellows and drowns it out, screaming, "I know! But it's going to kill us!"

> 66 To stop this ongoing cycle a way has to be found to calm the amygdala down and reprocess the event in its correct context. 99

As panicky ruminations and 're-living' of the event continue, these fresh arousals need to be discharged in the form of dreams – as the expectations aroused cannot be acted on, because the original traumatic event is in the past. And, because the event being dreamed about is so horrific, the dream is likely to be a nightmare and often one that is so vivid that it will wake the dreamer, who then remembers it. Then the nightmares too get added into the fear mix. (The explanation for dreaming is explained on page 41 in the generalised anxiety section.)

To stop this ongoing cycle, a way has to be found to calm the amygdala down and then reprocess and recodify the event, in its correct context. To do this, the trauma pattern needs to be reactivated briefly, but without allowing the amy-dala to get all excited and frightened again. Although this may sound impossible, it is in fact very simple to do. It is what happens in the rewind technique, which has been mentioned a few times already, and in other methods you may have heard of, such as Eye Movement Desensitisation Reprocessing (EMDR), Thought Field Therapy (TFT) and Emotional Freedom Therapy (EFT). In the rewind technique, the therapist first relaxes the person deeply, to calm them down, and then guides them through the traumatic experi-ence but in a dissociated (distanced) manner, which prevents arousal – they are invited to imagine themselves looking at a video or DVD of the traumatic event, which they are fast-forwarding, and then running backward through it, on fast rewind, as if they are in the event

> 66 ... the memory of the traumatic event no longer induces panic and intense fear ... 99

themselves. (The method is described in detail in Part 3). In EFT, the desired dissociation is achieved by asking the person to think about what happened and to re-experience their anx-iety but, at the same time, to tap certain parts of their face and body rhythmically in a certain order. In the other methods, something similar happens.

When the trauma is re-experienced in this dissociated, calm way, the hippocampus is no longer inhibited and can record the context as a safe one – the person is aware of sitting in the therapist's office, dealing with a memory. Because the brain is calmly processing the past trauma at the same time as it is processing the current situation of sitting in the room, the experience can be coded by the hippocampus as non-threatening – and the trauma memory is relegated to the past, where it should be. (This is rather like what happens when we wake in panic from a nightmare and realise that we are safe in bed. We immediately stop being fearful because a context has been created. *That* was a horrible dream, gone and finished. *This* is real life, now.)

So a new message is put into the person's memory and, while still in this state of low arousal, the therapist can engage the client's neocortex in drawing further distinctions between the traumatic but now non-threatening past event and present-day life. "The smell of petrol is normal at a petrol station, as you fill up your car and spill a little drop. It doesn't signify danger." "A great many people of all shapes and sizes, colours and creeds wear leather jackets. They are not all muggers." Thus a feedback loop is set in place, which allows the pattern in the amygdala to be reprogrammed. The memory of the traumatic event will always be an extremely unpleasant one, but it will no longer induce panic and intense fear or the feeling that it is happening now. The whole procedure can often be completed within 20 minutes, so is easy to do in a normal therapy session. (Of course, it can only work if the trauma is truly in the past. It cannot work, for instance, in cases of abuse that are ongoing.)

Arousing curiosity

Joe has suggested that these detraumatisation methods work so simply and quickly not because of magic or special knowledge but because they make use of a simple mechanism within the brain – one that brings us back to REM sleep again.*

The electrical signal described earlier, which draws our attention to any sudden movements and which fires off repeatedly when we dream, is not only known as the orientation response but also the PGO wave (for complicated reasons not worth bothering with here) and the curiosity reflex. We like the term curiosity reflex, so we'll use that one.

In dreaming, the curiosity reflex fires intensively while the day's emotionally arousing expectations that didn't get acted on, or completed in some way, are cleared out in dreams. As we have seen, we usually forget our dreams for the very good reason that if they became memories we would no longer be able to distinguish between what was real and what was purely metaphorical (see page 45). So, it seems, the curiosity reflex also triggers us to forget intense emotional memories. Even in waking life, inducing 'forgetting' is often the effect of

* Griffin, J. (2005). PTSD: Why some techniques for treating it work so fast. *Human Givens* Journal, 12, 2, 12–17

the curiosity reflex. Suppose you are chatting on the phone to a friend and there is a loud thud behind you. Instantly you whirl around, curious to identify the source, and see a precariously placed book has fallen off a table or a window blind has suddenly snapped up. When you turn back to your conversation, however, you might well find that you have completely forgotten what you were saying. The curiosity reflex has caused you to momentarily forget whatever was actively on your mind.

In evolutionary terms, this makes sense as a survival mechanism. When life was dangerous for us on a daily basis, we needed a mechanism that instantly drew our attention – and withdrew it completely from whatever we had been doing till that moment. You can't keep putting the finishing touches to your mammoth stew if a live wild boar's hot breath is nearly at your neck.

However, nor would we want to lose track of what we are doing every time something unexpected happens, as that would clearly also be a risk, not an aid, to survival. If we are making dinner or mending a bike or reading, and the distraction turns out to have been unimportant, we can easily get back to what we were doing, as the cooking utensils or the tools or the book remind us what it was. But it isn't so easy to remember what we were talking about or thinking, as we have nothing to orient ourselves by. That's why so many of us have the experience of setting off to get some item or other, being called or becoming engrossed in another thought, and then forgetting entirely what we had set out to get. This is often referred to in jest as 'a senior moment', but it happens to young people too. Any major distraction clears out our working (short-term) memory in case it is needed for something more important. After all, sometimes our survival does depend on a sudden switch of attention and total concentration.

During the rewind technique, a person is in a deeply relaxed state, which, in terms of what is happening in the brain, makes it easy for them to slip into the REM state. It makes sense, therefore, that, during the technique, the curiosity reflex would be triggered by the unfamiliar mental activity of imagining movements being run through backwards, thus causing temporary amnesia and clearing the fear pattern (which the therapist has deliberately aroused) out of consciousness. (In tapping, the curiosity reflex would be triggered by the tapping movements.) But the therapist has also established an expectation that the trauma will be resolved by this imagination exercise – and the neocortex is curious as to how. So, during the temporary amnesia, a good therapist will also take the opportunity to make suggestions that underline how the present situation is so very different from the trauma situation, and thus complete the neutralisation of the emotion that accompanied the memory.

We hope you are reassured by this explanation of PTSD and how and why it can be so easily and effectively treated by therapists trained in the rewind technique. (This is the method we favour over all others, for reasons we will explain in Part 3.)

Panic attacks

In many ways, panic attacks have much in common with a post-traumatic stress reaction. If you have experienced a full-blown panic attack, you might well rate it as the highest level of fear you could ever experience. Indeed, it is utterly terrifying and you will probably have been convinced you were dying. Because the experience is so catastrophic that it stays vividly in your mind and, when it happens again, and again, it is no surprise if your life starts to fall to pieces, as you do anything to avoid situations where panic might occur, and also are never quite sure that it won't happen in completely new, as yet unsuspected, situations and circumstances.

No doubt, if you suffer from panic attacks, you will have visited your doctor at some point, frightened that you have a heart condition or some other life-threatening illness; or you may have gone straight to the accident and emergency department at your local hospital where you were thoroughly checked out and told you were fine. But that didn't make sense because you know you weren't fine. *Something* had to be wrong. Or maybe you were told that you had had a panic attack, and that has made you worry that there is something wrong with you mentally. Why else would you go into what seems like a near-death state for no good reason at all?

> 66 ... you will then be able to prevent these attacks from happening altogether or from escalating, if they do. 99

Well, there *is* a good reason and when you understand how and why a panic attack takes hold, the fear can be taken out of it almost completely. You will then be able to learn how to prevent these attacks either from happening altogether or from escalating, if they do.

Warning!

IN A small number of cases, panic attacks can be triggered by a physical condition, such as heart and lung irregularities, an undiagnosed thyroid disorder, inner ear disturbance and epilepsy. They can also sometimes be triggered by side effects of prescribed drugs (particularly tranquillisers and anti-depressants), withdrawing from drugs, alcohol or smoking, or even by tight clothing that restricts breathing. It is best to see your doctor if you are concerned about possible causes. ●

Symptoms of panic explained

Let's look at some common symptoms of a panic attack. All of these symptoms are perfectly normal aspects of the fight-or-flight response that we unconsciously set in motion whenever we feel that we are under threat. (See page 12.)

- *Palpitations or sensation of a pounding heart:* our hearts pumps faster to cope with the increased demand that will be made on it, when we start fighting or running

- *Quick, shallow breathing:* we need to take in more oxygen quickly to increase our energy, thus fuelling our muscles so they can get moving and shift us out of this emergency quickly

- *Copious sweating:* our body is expecting to take some serious aerobic exercise (fighting or running for it), and we'll get too hot if we don't sweat

- *Sudden feeling of nausea and dry mouth:* this is because digestion stops when we are in an emergency situation, so that more blood can be diverted to the muscles in our arms and legs, to get us running faster

- *A sense of desperately needing to urinate or defecate:* again, this is to enable all available blood to go to the muscles in our legs and arms, the kidneys and intestines and bladder stop working, causing the muscles at the opening of the anus and bladder to relax.

Yet most people experience panic attacks in innocuous situations, like supermarkets or buses or any number of ordinary places that we might find ourselves in on an ordinary day – there is no evident threat and we aren't actually getting ready to run anywhere or fight anyone. And that is what leads to the rest of the frightening symptoms of a panic attack.

- **Sensations of shortness of breath, smothering and choking:** these horrible sensations are not imaginary! Unfortunately, because we *aren't* usually running anywhere or fighting, we can't use the extra oxygen we have just breathed in, in our short shallow breaths, so we breathe it out almost straight away and this has a significant effect.

Oxygen is a very sticky molecule and, without the aid of a gas called carbon dioxide, it sticks too closely to the red blood cells that carry it around to the various tissues in our bodies. This means it can't be readily released to be absorbed by the cells that need it. Normally, we breathe in the right amount of oxygen and, with the aid of carbon dioxide, this gets transferred to the body tissues, and then the carbon dioxide is breathed out. But when the oxygen is breathed out almost straight away, as a result of sustained shallow breathing but no action (hyperventilation), it takes precious carbon dioxide with it that hasn't done its job yet, causing the levels of available carbon dioxide in our blood to fall. Without the carbon dioxide to help, the remaining oxygen sticks to the red blood cells and we feel we are oxygen-starved, even though we are actually taking plenty in.

Most people naturally start gasping or panting when this happens,

> 66 Although the terrifying sensations of smothering or choking are all too real, neither would actually happen. 99

to take in more air to breathe, but unfortunately this has the opposite effect, because then even more carbon dioxide gets breathed out and even less oxygen is available for the body cells to get at. However, although the terrifying sensations of smothering or choking are all too real, neither would actually happen. The worst that could ever occur is that you would faint and then your breathing would return to normal – just as normally we breathe correctly automatically, without even thinking about it. It is the panic and the fear of dying that triggers and exacerbates the process that causes the conscious gasping and struggling to breathe.

- *Sharp chest pain:* again, this is real, not imaginary. But it is the result of strain on the chest muscles caused when you hyperventilate.

- *Trembling and shaking:* A little of this is the normal accompaniment of shallow breathing. But the more you hyperventilate, the stronger and more uncontrollable the trembling and shaking will be.

- *Dizziness or faintness:* the hyperventilating is to blame.

- *Numbness:* the hyperventilating is to blame.

- *Weakness:* again, the hyperventilating is to blame. The body is getting exhausted.

- *Difficulty speaking:* yet another result of hyperventilating.

- *Fear of losing control:* this is a realistic reaction. You have, unwittingly, turned on the fight-or-flight response to escape from danger and yet you are not escaping from danger. Every cell in your body is screaming for you to run or fight and you are staying put, so of course it feels as if you are losing control. But it is a feeling, not a reality. People have said to us, "But I *did* lose control. I was in the supermarket and I just put down my basket and fled." Our response is usually, "Did you leave by the door or the window? If you left by the door, you didn't lose control. You simply did the only thing you knew how to do that might possibly lower your panic."

- *A sense of being unreal:* people often find themselves thinking, "This can't be real. It's like a dream." They feel detached, as if they are looking at themselves going through this dreadful experience, and because of this they may jump to the conclusion that they are going insane. But this sense of dissociation is again just a natural defence mechanism in the circumstances, an attempt to lower the soaring arousal and calm yourself down. (We make positive use of this natural mechanism for the same purpose, in treatment.)

■ *You think you are dying:* with all the alarming, escalating physical symptoms that you are experiencing, it is no wonder that you fear you are dying, if you don't understand what, physically, is going on!

So, amazingly, all this results from hyperventilating. If you were to breathe noisily through your open mouth now for two minutes, you would get these very same symptoms. (There is more carbon dioxide loss through an open mouth than through the narrower outlet of the nostrils.) We don't suggest you do this but we do sometimes suggest it to our patients – as we are there to calm them down again – so that they can see for themselves.

It would all be over in moments if ...

A panic attack, then, is just nature's normal response to the perception of a strong physical or emotional threat and it would burn itself out within probably two or three minutes, if left to follow its natural course. Fight or flight symptoms will always naturally peak within 10 minutes at most. (If symptoms last for hours, you are not having a panic attack.)

The only reason symptoms *don't* peak quickly when we are having a panic attack is because our terrified thoughts and dire imaginings lead us to hyperventilate and thus increase and perpetuate the symptoms. In effect, we are frightening ourselves half to death! Our bodies aren't doing it. It is fuelled by our imagination and such thoughts as:

"My chest! I'm having a heart attack!"

"It has never been this bad before. I know it was only a panic attack last time but this time it has really got to be a heart attack!"

"I can't move my tongue. I'm having a stroke!"

"Why am I sweating like this? I must be seriously ill."

"I can't breathe!"

"What am I doing here? I don't remember getting here."

"I'm going to be sick! I'm going to disgrace myself! Oh, I couldn't stand the embarrassment!"

The symptoms of a panic attack are understandably frightening if you don't know what's causing them, whereas understanding can make all the difference. Some people find that the explanatory information we have provided here is all they need to enable them to gain control over such unhelpful thoughts. When they know that their bodies are, in fact,

> 66 Understanding what causes your symptoms can make all the difference ... 99

reacting in a natural way to some highly stressful situation, and that they aren't going to die, they can stop churning up the action with panicky thoughts.

But what's so threatening about a supermarket?

Imagine this scenario. *Jenny is a single mother of a three-year-old and a baby girl. Today, as usual, she has dropped off Alex, her three-year-old, for his morning session at nursery school and then she has raced into town to try to get her errands done before she needs to return to pick him up. She goes to the post office and the shoe repair shop. She doesn't dare go into the bank – she is overdrawn and really worried about how she is going to handle her financial problems. She is just about to set off back to the nursery when she remembers that she is out of ketchup. If Alex doesn't have ketchup – and it has to be a particular brand of ketchup – with his lunch, he will have one of his monster tantrums, and Jenny just can't cope. She is already chronically sleep-deprived as it is, what with the baby waking up several times in the night and Alex coming in to her early in the morning. Will she have time to dart into the supermarket, pick up a bottle of ketchup and get out quickly in the hand basket queue? She decides to risk it, as the tantrum alternative is so unthinkable today.*

She grabs the bottle and makes straight for the quick checkout. There are two people ahead of her, but they don't have much in their baskets. But there does seem to be a problem at the front of the queue.

A customer is arguing with the cashier about something or other. Jenny starts to get anxious about the time. If she is late and Alex is the last child left, that will bring on another tantrum and she will virtually have to drag him down the road, with everyone looking at her, thinking her a terrible mother. The customer is still arguing. The cashier is just shrugging her shoulders. Jenny can feel herself getting tense. Then the cashier puts on her light, to signal for a supervisor. Jenny looks around. There is no supervisor in sight. Her anxiety is soaring. And then she remembers that Alex's teacher has already told her off several times for being late and had said that, if it happened again, she might have to call social services, because she couldn't be expected to give up her short lunch hour to look after other people's children ...!

Suddenly, Jenny feels a stabbing pain. She can't catch her breath. She can't breathe ...!

And no doubt you can picture the rest of the story.

There is, of course, nothing inherently threatening about supermarkets or any other innocent places in which panic attacks occur. They just happen to be the places you are in when an intolerable load of stresses, put together, suddenly rise above the level that you can cope with. For Jenny, this was a combination of coping alone with a very young family, being sleep-deprived, having financial worries and fearing the consequences of being late to pick up her child. She was only conscious of the last concern at the time. But our friend the amygdala had other ideas. It sensed the emotional temperature rocketing, diagnosed highly probable danger, set the fight-or-flight response in motion – and the result is a panic attack.

But that, alas, is not the end of it. As a panic attack is such a terrifying experience, the amygdala will definitely file away the information for future pattern-matching purposes. As it works with sensory knowledge, it won't be interested in all of the circumstances that led to Jenny's collapse. It will only register the fact that she was in a bright, busy place, where people were queueing. And so, on another occasion, even though Alex and the baby are with their grandmother and an unexpected windfall has sorted her finances out, Jenny has another panic attack while standing in a post office queue.

Even when someone knows there was a clear cause for their first panic attack – for instance, they felt sick whilst taking an exam and hadn't dared to ask to rush out to the toilet – that doesn't stop it from happening again, if the original predicament produced enough panic. The amygdala has noted the occasion – being shut in a room where people are working silently – and the next panic attack occurs in the local library. And so it goes on, with new features of each situation noted by the amygdala, to serve as further triggers for raising the alarm the next time. (We will consider the full consequences of this shortly, when we look at agoraphobia.)

Smoke alarms and washing machines

When people don't understand what a panic attack is and why it is happening to them, they often think they are having 'a nervous breakdown'. But nerves don't break down. That idea comes from a quaint metaphor coined around the time that telephones were invented. After all, nerves could be considered to be a bit like telephone cables and cables break down. But there the slim similarity ends.

However, a good metaphor does provide a helpful way of getting a handle on complex events. And we think that there are much better metaphors for understanding panic attacks. For instance, a panic attack that occurs when there is no actual emergency is a rather

> **A panic attack when there is no emergency is like an overly sensitive smoke alarm ...**

like a smoke alarm that is so sensitive that it sometimes goes off even when there isn't a fire. Everyone wonders what is happening for a moment or two but then they realise they can just safely turn it off. Nothing dire happens as a result.

Or maybe a panic attack is like the fast spin in a washing machine. Just as your washing machine is designed to spin and vibrate and withstand all that sudden activity at certain times in the washing cycle, so your heart and your body are designed to thump and shake when you get highly aroused. Normally you would run like the clappers as a result but, if there is nothing to run from and if you don't keep repeatedly pressing the 'spin' button (i.e. think frightening thoughts), your arousal will settle down again quickly of its own accord. Easier said than done, of course, but in Part 2 we will show you how. The rewind technique, which is so successful in resolving symptoms of post-traumatic stress, is also highly effective in bringing down the emotional arousal associated with past panic attacks (see Part 3).

Agoraphobia

The term agoraphobia literally means fear of the market place (from the Greek) but is used to mean fear of busy, crowded places, which markets, of course, usually are. It tends to blend with claustrophobia (fear of enclosed places), although one can be claustrophobic without being agoraphobic.

Agoraphobia is a self-protective response to the fear of panic attacks (see above). Most people with agoraphobia have experienced many terrifying, seemingly inexplicable panic attacks and, as a consequence, want to stay at home as much as possible, to try to prevent them happening or to feel less unsafe if they do, and to have someone with them if they go out. This is perfectly natural. Once the amygdala gets in on the act and is in hyper-alert survival mode, it patterns matches to events and experiences that have only remote connections with the source of a panic. As we saw with Jenny, understandably panicky feelings in the supermarket queue that were misinterpreted led to another panic attack in the post office. Quite possibly, she would have gone on to have another attack in a place where there were a lot of people, but not necessarily queueing, such as while she was standing on a crowded train or a bus. Maybe the person in front of her there, whom she was terrified of collapsing or vomiting upon, was wearing a pink coat with a fur collar. Then perhaps another day, when she was in the familiar little local park with her children at a nice quiet time, she had yet another, seemingly incomprehensible, attack – one of the other mums was wearing a pink coat with a fur collar. Jenny may not consciously have remembered the pink coat, but her amygdala has ...

In such circumstances, when it suddenly seems that anytime and anywhere, these terrifying attacks can happen out of the blue, what can be more normal than wanting to stay at home, where you feel safer? What can be more normal than wanting to have someone with you to help you, if circumstances force you to go out? It is a response that dates back to our evolutionary past, when we were vulnerable to dangerous animal predators. After all, we had very few natural defence mechanisms available to us. We didn't have sharp talons or huge jaws to use to defend ourselves, if we felt under threat. So our instincts were to retreat to our caves when scared and to gang up on whatever was attacking us (i.e. have someone else alongside). These are absolutely natural responses to environmental threats. The only problem is that, nowadays, mostly, the environment isn't really threatening. Our amygdala is responding to the wrong signals.

But this doesn't mean a life sentence. It can be straightforward to correct, once you know how.

Some other common phobias

A phobia is an irrational fear that is so strong that it induces enormous anxiety or panic (often a panic attack too) and a strong desire to avoid encountering the feared creature, circumstance or substance. If you suffer from a phobia you will probably be aware that your fear is unwarranted, unreasonable and totally out of proportion to the situation, but you are unable to control it, and so it gets in the way of your living a normal life. Some phobias can make life miserable.

It is possible to develop a phobia about absolutely anything. Indeed, the existence of technical names for obscure ones – such as stasiphobia (standing upright), siderophobia (stars), ommatophobia (eyes) and nephophobia (clouds), to mention just a few – suggests that at least some people at some time have developed phobias about the most unlikely things. However, the most common ones, besides agoraphobia and claustrophobia, are fear of spiders, snakes, worms, flying, heights and various social phobias (which we'll look at separately in a moment). Other not uncommon ones include bird feathers, blood and injections. More than one in 10 people suffer from a phobia at some time, and women are twice as likely to do so as men.

As might be expected from what we have covered so far, people can develop phobic responses to any situation, animal or substance associated (consciously or not) with a circumstance in which they have previously experienced acute panic – the amygdala in action again. Jenny, for instance, could quite easily have developed a phobia about pink coats. Someone else might develop a phobia about grass if they were in a newly mown garden the first time they experienced a panic attack.

> 66 It doesn't matter if you have no idea where your original terror came from. 99

Sometimes the fear is quite understandable at the start. A child is set upon by an aggressive dog, perhaps. But then this develops into a fear of all dogs and may even widen so that the person is frightened of seeing dogs on the television or even pictures of them in books or magazines. Sometimes children learn their fears from their parents. If your mother screamed and hid every time there was a clap of thunder or stood on the table screeching if a daddy long-legs crossed the floor, it is little surprise if you develop a fear of thunderstorms and creepy-crawlies too.

Maybe you have no idea where your terror came from. The good news is, it doesn't matter. All that is important is that the learned association between the thing and the fear is broken. This can be easily done. We show you, in Part 2, what you can do to break it and also, in Part 3, how a therapist can help you to do it, quickly and painlessly.

Social phobias

The variety of forms that social phobias take can also be explained in terms of our biology.

The most common social phobias are fear of speaking in public; fear of writing in public; fear of blushing; and fear of eating in public. At the heart of them all is the fear of being judged negatively. If we look at these situational fears individually, we can see that they are focused on one or other aspects of the normal fight-or-flight response, which is triggered in stressful situations.

For instance, a phobia about eating in public can often develop as a result of experiencing a panic attack in a restaurant. One person might become hyper-aware of the choking sensation that occurs when oxygen doesn't reach the tissues, because of shallow breathing; another might become hyper-aware that their saliva has dried up and their throat muscles are constricted, literally making it impossible to eat. Both of these aspects of a panic attack could understandably lead to a fear of eating in public.

Another physiological aspect of the panic response is the sensation that our tongue isn't working and we are unable to speak properly. Of course, when we are very highly aroused, we cannot think straight either. All this could easily translate into a fear of speaking in public, whether giving a presentation to colleagues or a speech at your best friend's wedding.

We also shake when we are panicked. Having that experience when eyes are upon us can easily lead to a fear of doing anything in public that might draw attention to our hands – such as writing a cheque.

A lot of people fear blushing. Yet this again is a natural part of the fight-or-flight response – blood rushes to the face. When blood courses through the muscles of the face, we see it as 'blushing'. But, of course, blushing occurs all over the body when we are aroused; it's just that, normally, we are only aware of the face and neck area.

So different social phobias arise, as a result of our focusing on one particular aspect of the whole cascade of fight-or-flight responses, rather than another.

Joe once treated a young doctor who had developed a phobia about eating in public after an occasion when he was having a meal in a restaurant with a friend. The doctor saw a couple of people he knew and noticed that they were looking at him and then speaking together as if they were discussing him. He was already in a highly vulnerable state, as his girl-

> **"** ... blushing is yet again a natural part of the fight-or-flight response and actually occurs all over the body. **"**

friend had very recently broken off their engagement. That was devastating enough. But now he assumed that she must have told these people about it, and they were looking at him and laughing at him for getting dumped. He began to feel extremely self-conscious and anxious. As he went to swallow the food in his mouth, he found he had no saliva and so really did start to choke. And then everyone in the restaurant was looking at him.

After that, he couldn't eat in a restaurant again. But then he soon found that he couldn't eat in the hospital canteen either. And then he started avoiding pubs, in case people offered peanuts around and he might feel obliged to take some. By the time he came to see Joe, he couldn't even drink a cup of coffee in the presence of another person, and his whole social life had collapsed. Not only was he fearful a great deal of the time but he had also become increasingly withdrawn and lonely. Fortunately, Joe was able to cure him very quickly by the means described later in the book, which can be used for all social phobias.

A phobia about speaking in public is very often triggered by a bad experience of being made to read aloud to the class, when a child at school. Children who feel nervous naturally find their mouths going dry and the words coming out funny, so their fear of doing badly is confirmed by the reality – and, to compound their shame, they are often laughed at or told off by their teacher, to boot. Such an experience can cause a lasting fear of performing in public, unless addressed.

Another common trigger of this particular fear is temperamental shyness. Some people are, by nature, more introverted than others. But that doesn't mean that shy people can't learn to be skilful speakers, or to enjoy social gatherings; it just means they have to work a bit harder at it. (If children are shy, it is enormously helpful to encourage them to take speech and drama classes; they learn confidence and social skills that make the process so much easier. Natural introverts never stop being introverted but they can manage their temperament instead of their temperament managing them.)

Obsessive-compulsive behaviour

At least three per cent of people suffer from obsessive-compulsive disorders (OCD), a miserable condition in which one's life can virtually be taken over by frightening, intrusive, repetitive thoughts, images or impulses and the resulting urgent need to perform specific actions, to ward off harm or to make things 'all right'. There is also a tendency to continually seek reassurance that everything will be okay. The most common obsessive-compulsive behaviours are repeated hand washing and 'checking' activities – for instance, checking a number of times that the back door is locked or that the gas is turned off.

As we said earlier, there are many, many different ways that people respond to levels of stress that are higher than they can cope with, and OCD is just one of them. For the most common trigger for obsessive-compulsive behaviours is a steep rise in stress, which could have any number of causes – from a debilitating physical illness, say, or getting a fright or not getting enough sleep to relationship breakdown, exam worries or money problems. Sometimes a person's stress levels may creep up almost unnoticed and it is one small, final stress that acts as the proverbial straw that breaks the camel's back. Whatever the cause, the result is worrisome thoughts: sufferers fear that a loved one will die or that their house will be repossessed or that they themselves will inflict harm on someone else. Often, however, the thought seems to have no relationship to anything that is actually concerning them. It just seems like a mad idea, which has arrived out of the blue. Unsurprisingly, such thoughts cause the individual great anxiety and gradually a compulsive activity develops, as an attempt to compensate or block the malign power of the thought.

Sometimes there is an evident link between the alarming thoughts and the compulsive activity – for instance, it is reasonable that someone with high anxiety about picking up other people's germs and getting ill might try to alleviate this risk by washing their hands. But sometimes there is no obvious link: for instance, a woman might suddenly think, out of the blue, "I'm going to kill my son!" and then feel the desperate need to perform complex mental calculations in some particular order to 'disempower' the thought.

> 66 It is extremely common for people to have momentary, highly disturbing thoughts. 99

It is worth mentioning here that, according to research, it is extremely common for people to have momentary, highly disturbing thoughts such as, "I could hurt my child" or "I think I might push the person in front of me on to the track, when the train comes in" – when the person whom the thought is about has done nothing whatso-

ever to provoke it. Very often such thoughts, which are usually fleeting, reflect a fear of inadequacy (e.g. hurting one's
child because one isn't a good enough mother) or fear of loss
of control or behaving unacceptably in public (with murder
certainly being the most extreme example of that!) Someone
who goes on to suffer from obsessive-compulsive behaviours,
however, may be particularly shocked by such thoughts and
be less able than others to dismiss them. Dwelling on them
and worrying about them inevitably make such thoughts all
the more likely to come to mind again and harder to ignore,
until eventually rituals are generated as a means of compen-
sating for them.

Sufferers from OCD know that what they are doing is irrational. Yet this doesn't in any way help to stop them needing
to put clothes in a certain order in the wardrobe to ensure
someone doesn't die in a car accident; or from needing to
return home, despite having already covered several miles of
a journey, just to check once again that the front door is locked
or that the alarm is set properly. For the fear generated if the
ritual cannot be carried out is almost unbearable. And it
grows. Terrifying thoughts about germs may become so insis-
tent for someone that, instead of washing their hands vigor-
ously just once or twice a day, the ritual has to be *performed*
50 times a day or for periods of longer and longer duration, in
a set pattern and uninterrupted – should someone enter the

room, the whole procedure may have to be started again from scratch. In fact, sufferers commonly say that they lose all track of time while carrying out their rituals, unaware, for instance, that they have been washing their hands for an hour. They are in a trance state. And in such a state, they may find that they can't remember whether they have carried out the ritual 'properly' and thus have to repeat it again, and again. In these ways, as you may well have experienced, OCD takes over lives. Research shows that even when people without OCD repeatedly check that something important has been

Has my child got OCD?

MOST OF us, as children, will have developed certain rituals, such as not stepping on the cracks in the pavement or needing to see three red cars in a row, designed to 'ensure' that we will get our maths right that day or that we won't get into trouble. At a certain level, such rituals are known to be a game, and not being able to carry them out does not cause anxiety. More importantly, they are seen as fun. If a little girl enjoys lining up her soft cuddly toys in a particular order at the end of her bed, she does not have OCD. If a little boy likes running to pat every tree he passes on the walk to school, he does not have OCD. Obsessive-compulsive activities are never enjoyable, for the very fact that they *are* compulsions. No one enjoys doing what they feel compelled to do.

done, they become less and less certain that they have actually done it.*

Some people manage to keep their obsessive-compulsive behaviour a secret from family and friends, even though it takes up more and more of their time and energy. Others, because of the nature of the compulsion, cannot hide what is happening. Either way, there are commonly strong accompanying feelings of helplessness and guilt.

The worst thing, of course, is that carrying out the ritual *doesn't* get rid of the intrusive, frightening, unacceptable

PANDA – a specific cause of OCD

IT HAS only relatively recently been realised that throat infections, caused by the bacterium streptococcus, can sometimes trigger obsessive-compulsive symptoms in children, as well as tics (odd, repetitive movements). This is now known as paediatric autoimmune neuropsychiatric disorder (PANDA). Researchers have found that antibodies produced in response to the infection 'cross react' with proteins in a part of the brain that is implicated in movement disorders. When the immune system has dealt with the infection, the OCD usually remits. However, the symptoms can return any time another such infection is suffered. PANDA has been identified in children aged 3–14. In some cases, plasma transfusions have successfully been used to deal with the disorder.

* Radomsky, A.S., Gilchrist, P. T. and Dussault, D. (2006). Repeated checking really does cause memory distrust, *Behaviour Research and Therapy*, 44, 305–316

thought. Even though sufferers know that, and may constantly tell themselves that they will not perform the compulsive
act, they just cannot prevent themselves – for reasons we will
explain. And that brings us back to the amygdala again. This
tiny organ plays a huge role in keeping OCD going. Understanding how it does this will help us understand how to
break the pattern.

OCD is like an addiction

As we have seen, the amygdala stores our unconscious emotional memories and matches any new experiences to these. If
something is recognised as safe, because we've experienced it
without any problem before, then all is well and our amygdala can relax. If a current experience matches one perceived
as dangerous or life threatening, however, it sets off the alarm
at once, and action gets taken. This is also what happens with
the intrusive thoughts or images: the amygdala recognises a
threat and raises the alarm, and so the ritual is initiated, to
dissipate it. And, because there is an *expectation* that carrying
out the ritual will deal with the threatening thought, the 'connection' between the two is embedded all the more deeply.
Yet, as we know, this expectation is *not* fulfilled. Although the
stress caused by the thought is temporarily reduced after the
ritual, the thought soon resurfaces, followed each time by
more ritual. So why, then, does the expectation persist?

Suppose Kate has the repetitive intrusive thought that her son will die in a car accident that day, unless, each time she has the thought, she remakes his bed from scratch 10 times. But today, desperate to get free of the compulsion and knowing in her heart of hearts that it will make no difference, she firmly resolves not to carry out the ritual the next time the thought occurs.

The part of her brain that makes that decision is technically termed the *dorsolateral prefrontal cortex* but we'll call it 'the boss'.* When the fearful thought comes into Kate's mind, her amygdala registers it, pattern matches to danger, as usual, and sets off the alarm that usually leads automatically to the bed-making ritual. But this time the boss says, "No, let's ignore it." The amygdala is flabbergasted. There must be some mistake. So it sends an SOS to an area of the brain known as the *anterior cingulate*, which we'll call 'the boss's secretary'* (as the boss's secretary is usually the one who really holds all the power). The message, begging to do the ritual, is sent in the form of a chemical cocktail. This includes a chemical called dopamine, which creates motivation and the desire to act. In effect, the presence of dopamine is like putting a priority sticker on the message. At this point, Kate

---

* We developed our idea of the boss and the boss's secretary from John Ratey's concept of 'the chief executive officer' and 'the executive secretary' to describe the dorsolateral prefrontal cortex and the anterior cingulated structures in the brain. See Ratey, J. (2001). *A User's Guide to the Brain*. Little, Brown and Company.

is experiencing just mild anxiety about not carrying out her ritual, because that is the effect of the small amount of dopamine that the amygdala can muster.

When the boss's secretary gets the message, however, she is confused – the amygdala has never had to involve her in this set of circumstances before. So she acts at once to get more information on the matter. She in turn sends a message, this time to the hippocampus. This is the organ that we discussed in the context of PTSD and which, among other things, stores all of the memories from the near or distant past that we can recall at will. The message the hippocampus receives is a request for any memories that will throw light on the current situation. So the hippocampus sends back a 'file' showing how consistently terrible the experience of the intrusive thought has been and how the only way to get it out of mind and to stop terrible harm happening has been to carry out the bed-making ritual.

Horrified at the apparent danger Kate is in, the boss's secretary hastily scribbles out a letter granting permission to do the ritual, puts it in one of her 'highest priority' envelopes (i.e. adds a massive amount more dopamine to the chemical message) and brings it through to the boss for an instant signature. And, although the boss had resolved not to do the ritual, when he receives the message with all its dopamine, the desire to take action (do the ritual) is so overwhelming that he gives in, thus Kate rushes to remake the bed.

The key to recovery from OCD is in *changing* the dopamine-soaked expectation. Obsessive-compulsive disorders are exactly like addictions, because both involve repeating behaviours that actually belie our expectations.* It is the dopamine that deceives us, by making the memory of the experience of carrying out the ritual (or smoking a cigarette or drinking 10 pints of beer) far better than it ever really was. Both rely on magical thinking: life will be wonderful if I have a cigarette or a drink; my son will be safe if I remake his bed 10 times. But rituals *don't* make the world a safer place, any more than cigarettes and drink ever really make life wonderful.

As we saw, when the amygdala first gets involved, there is only mild anxiety. It is only the *expectation* that dire consequences will follow if Kate doesn't do the ritual that keeps the whole thing going. Without that, the anxiety or fear would not be overwhelming, and Kate could learn ways to cope with it. So what needs to be done is to intervene at the point where the boss's secretary sends to the hippocampus for memories – and call up very different ones (such as "I feel just as fearful again a few minutes after I remake the bed. And I feel full of guilt after doing it, because I then don't have time to do other important things that really matter") that *won't* strike the

* For a full account of the expectation theory of addiction, see our book *Freedom from Addiction: The secret behind successful addiction busting* (HG Publishing, East Sussex).

boss's secretary as necessary to act on, and so she won't even bother the boss with them. (We'll explain in Part 2 about how to work with this information.)

Psychosis

Clearly, high anxiety and stress can cause all sorts of problems for us. But in some rare cases they can even lead to psychosis, an extreme mental state in which delusions and/or hallucinations occur and thought processes may be altered. Elsewhere, we have suggested that psychosis is waking reality processed through the dreaming brain,* and this has resonated with many people who have suffered from psychosis. "It was like living in the weirdest dream," they have told us. When we are dreaming, we are in the REM state. And when we experience bizarre events in dreams, we often at the time don't even find them odd. We are also less sensitive to pain or to other sensations (for instance, we don't feel uncomfortable at the time but might on waking, if one of our arms is trapped in an awkward position). And, if someone calls to us while we are asleep, their voice may be incorporated into our dream, thus appearing to be inside our own heads. All of this mirrors the altered reality, delusions, hallucinations and desensitisation that occur in psychosis too.

---

* Griffin, J. and Tyrrell, I. (2001). Trapped in the land of illusion. *Human Givens Journal*, 8, 3, 2.

As explained earlier, when anxious thoughts are bombarding the brain, the need to discharge them through REM sleep is exacerbated. This leads to longer and more intense periods of REM sleep, in effect damaging the REM sleep mechanism. In cases of extreme stress and anxiety, it is conceivable that the damage could be even more pronounced, and that an individual could be dipping in and out of the REM state when awake. Although anxiety and stress may rarely result in psychosis, psychosis is almost always preceded by stress.

For instance, Joe once treated a man called Vic who had begun to hallucinate that his wife had turned into his mother. It didn't take Joe long to find out that Vic was under considerable stress at work and this, in turn, was putting his marriage under strain. Whenever his wife got angry with him or he felt she was nagging him, the hallucination occurred. Vic had had a very difficult relationship with his mother, who had been extremely controlling.

Joe suggested to Vic that he was experiencing dream phenomena, brought on by stress. He was pattern matching to images of his mother when his wife behaved in certain ways but, because his heightened stress pushed him into a waking REM state at such times, he *experienced* his wife as his mother instead of just being reminded of her. This explanation reduced Vic's anxiety considerably and he was able, with Joe's help, to calm down and address the stresses he was under in a practical way.

Drugs are not the answer to anxiety

Medication for anxiety disorders can be helpful in emergencies, if you really, really think you can't cope for another minute, or you haven't had any sleep for nights. But sleeping pills (which are just reformulations of tranquillisers) induce lower quality sleep and we quickly habituate to them. After three nights, they don't work any more, and we get at best only 15 minutes more sleep with them than without them. As for other tranquillising drugs or antidepressants, they may appear to calm us down for a while but, more often than not, the dosage has to keep being upped, because they soon cease to do the job so well.

Plenty of studies have compared the effectiveness of drug treatment and psychotherapeutic treatments for different anxiety disorders and these have overwhelmingly shown that drugs offer no long-term answer. One meta-analysis* (a review of a large number of studies) found that there was no advantage to adding drugs to effective behaviour therapy but that effective behaviour therapy added to drug treatment could increase effectiveness by half.

> 66 The key is to look at what is missing from our lives ... 99

Unfortunately, despite the research findings, both tranquil-

---

* Danton, W., Antonuccio, D. and Rosenthal, Z. (1997) No need to panic, *The Therapist*, 4,4, 38–40.

lisers and antidepressants are still being prescribed for anxiety. And that's on top of the excess of drugs, such as caffeine, alcohol, cigarettes and cannabis, that many people already use in a vain attempt to cope with stress. But taking drugs for anxiety is not nearly as effective as finding out what is causing the anxiety in the first place. By looking at what is missing from our lives, and then learning how to get back on track by doing something about it, we can make real, long-lasting changes.

This is what the human givens approach is all about.

The human givens

Every living thing needs the right nourishment from its environment to be healthy. And every living thing knows how to get that nourishment. Plants 'know' they must turn to the sun, to be able to produce the chlorophyll they need to make their food; their roots 'know' to suck up moisture from the soil. Babies know to seek the nipple (or bottle teat) for food; they know how to build rapport with their main carers (by being responsive, smiling, etc.), to ensure that they are taken care of, and so on. All living things have an innate 'guidance system' like this to help them get their essential needs met. Our essential needs and the innate guidance system we were gifted with to help us meet them together form 'the human givens'.

Essential emotional needs

We all need food, water, warmth and shelter from the elements in order to survive – these are basic 'givens'. But there are many other needs, emotional rather than physical, that are equally crucial for our wellbeing – and sometimes even for our survival too. Decades of health and social research have shown that these include:

- security – a sense of being safe, which enables us to lead our lives without undue fear

- a sense of autonomy and control over our lives

- attention – receiving it from others, but also giving it

- emotional connection to other people – friendship, love, intimacy, fun

- connection to the wider community – being part of something larger than ourselves

- privacy – to reflect

- a sense of status – being accepted and valued in the different social groups we belong to

- a sense of our own competence and achievement – which ensures we don't suffer from 'low self-esteem'

- a sense of meaning and purpose – which comes from doing things that mentally and/or physically stretch us.

Our innate guidance system

To help us find ways to meet our needs, nature has given us a wealth of resources, such as:

- the ability to add new knowledge to our innate knowledge: to learn and remember

- the ability to build rapport, empathise and connect with others

- a powerful imagination, to aid problem solving

- the ability to think things out, analyse, plan and adapt

- the ability to understand the world unconsciously – through pattern matching

- the ability to step back into our 'observing self' (our self-awareness) – and be objective

- the ability to dream and thus discharge any unexpressed emotionally arousing expectations, so that we can face each day afresh.

These needs and resources together – the human givens – are in-built patterns, or biological templates, which direct our actions and responses. If a person is thriving and having their needs met, in appropriate balance, they cannot suffer from anxiety disorders or any other mental disorder.

What, then, could prevent us from getting our needs met? There are only three possibilities, and all mental distress is due to one or a combination of these.

POSSIBILITY 1:
The environment doesn't provide the nourishment needed

For instance, children that are emotionally or physically abused by their parents, or whose parents are emotionally distant or too authoritarian or too liberal, or constantly critical, cannot be mentally healthy in that setting. They are harmfully conditioned by the experience. Likewise, adults that are bullied at work or stressed by unrealistic targets and deadlines cannot be mentally healthy in that work environment.

POSSIBILITY 2:
The innate guidance system has become damaged

This could be because of genetic damage or physical damage (for instance, a head injury) but most commonly it is because of psychological damage: trauma. This could take the form of PTSD or be less extreme, yet still affect the way we function in the world. Addictions, too, can corrupt the way that the guidance system works – substituting destructive impulses for life-enhancing drives.

POSSIBILITY 3:
The innate guidance system isn't being used properly

The more complex an organism is, the more learning is involved in operating the guidance system correctly. For instance, babies may have the ability to build initial rapport, by the very fact of being endearing, vulnerable little creatures that inspire love and caring in the adults connected with them. But that isn't enough. As they grow into children and then adults, they need to know how to be social animals – to make the right social responses, to make friends, to build intimate and professional relation-ships, to develop the ability to learn

> **66** Whatever the reason for your anxiety, there is much that can be done to relieve the distress **99**

and use information, to make shrewd judgements, to trust wisely, to be self-assertive, to manage stress, and so on. If we don't have these life skills, albeit through no fault of our own, we cannot get our needs met fully. For instance, if our parents were cruel or uncaring, we may find it hard to trust others or create close relationships. If we were laughed at when we made a mistake at school, we may not develop confidence in our abilities.

Sometimes we use aspects of the guidance system incor-rectly. As we have seen, imagination, which is a powerful aid in problem solving, is heavily misused (unwittingly, of course) by people with anxiety, who spend so much time imagining dire outcomes of one kind or another (worrying, in other words) that they may prevent themselves from being able to problem solve at all.

But whatever the reason for your own high levels of anxi-ety (or that of whoever you are trying to help), there is much that can be done to relieve the distress and take back control of your life. When human givens therapists work with people suffering from anxiety disorders, we first look to see which important needs are not being met in their lives and/or which of their innate resources are either not being used or are being used incorrectly. We then help each individual to build up effective ways to meet their needs, at the same time as they are learning how to handle high anxiety.

These are the techniques we are going to share with you in the next chapter.

PART 2

Overcoming anxiety

*H*AVING looked in detail at what happens to us when we become anxious, we can now get down to the business of tackling anxiety. The first 15 sections of this chapter will teach you vital skills for dealing with it. These are crucial not just for overcoming generalised anxiety, but for reducing vulnerability to the other forms too. We will also be looking individually at what you can do to handle specific forms of anxiety. But as post-traumatic stress and most phobias are best treated by therapists, and can in fact be completely cured, we will cover them separately in Part 3.

So, to recap quickly, there are three elements to any anxiety disorder. These are:

- **physiological** *(tension, inability to relax, disturbed sleep, etc.)*
- **emotional** *(imagining catastrophe, sense of apprehension, anticipatory fear, etc.)*
- **cognitive** *(negative thoughts, poor concentration, etc.).*

Throughout the following pages, we will help you to deal with all of them.

Learn how to relax

The first thing anyone who suffers from anxiety needs to do is learn a reliable, pleasant way to relax. Of course, if you suffer from anxiety, relaxing – or being able to calm yourself at vital moments – is probably the very thing that you find hardest to do. But the ability to calm down, relax, or mentally and physically take time out (whatever you choose to call it) is an absolutely key weapon in the arsenal you are now going to assemble to tackle your over-anxiety and recapture your mental equilibrium.

Relaxing is important not just because high anxiety is a horrible, exhausting and often frightening feeling, but because, when you are anxious, you are highly emotionally aroused and, as we have seen, in that state – however hard you try – you cannot think straight. The emotional brain strong-arms its way centre stage, pushing the rational part of your brain out into the wings or off-stage altogether, leaving you at the mercy of primitive, emotional, black-or-white thinking such as, "I'll die if I have to do that!" "I'm having a heart attack!" "I'll never be good enough!" It is these types of thoughts that crank up our emotional temperature and send anxiety soaring.

As we have already observed, we all need access to anxious feelings to keep us alert to dangers and to motivate us to take on new challenges. But, to deal with unproductive, self-defeating anxiety, we also need our sense of perspective back, so that we can look at the whole picture; if we are highly emotionally aroused, we can't even begin to do that.

Calming anxious people down – and teaching them how to do it for themselves – is a priority in a first human givens therapy session. Most people find this an enormously helpful – and enjoyable – experience. It is like being given permission to let go of all that agonising and ruminating, checking and worrying, so that you can just appreciate being in your own body for a moment, often for the first time in a long while.

You may be feeling doubtful that you will ever be able to relax again, but we have never come across anyone who couldn't be helped to relax at least for a little while, even those who were utterly convinced that it couldn't be done, or were actively resistant. However, we don't force people to relax 'our way'. What works is to find the way that does

> **66** Things <u>can</u> be different and you <u>can</u> make changes happen. **99**

the magic for you. And there will be one. For your body will be yearning for relief from the highly unnatural state of un-relenting stress you may unwittingly be subjecting yourself to. Ten or 15 or 30 minutes' calm is a wonderful gift to give yourself. It will show you, through the very experience of changes you can induce in your own body, that things *can* be different; you *can* make changes happen.

Once you know what true relaxation feels like (many people tell us that they had quite forgotten), you will soon become able to relax yourself quickly whenever you need to. (It's like coming into money and being able to afford to take a mini-break whenever you need to 'recharge your batteries'.) This is a brilliantly effective way of preventing anxiety from escalating into a panic attack or a fearful thought from leading to a compulsive activity – it leaves you access to the full power of your thinking brain, so that you can put your situation into perspective and defuse it on the spot.

A few ways to relax quickly

Here are a few easy and effective methods you can use to induce relaxation – choose one you like or try them all out, and then practise the one you like best for 10 minutes at least twice a day. If you are unable to relax by yourself at the beginning, it could help if you see a therapist so that they can do a guided relaxation with you. We often tape such sessions, so that clients can replay the tape and induce a relaxed state whenever they want to. Alternatively, you might like to ask someone to read the steps to you for the first few times, so that you can focus on relaxing.

1. The 7/11 method

Many people find that the easiest way to relax is to concentrate on their own breathing, so we suggest you try this method first. (If paying attention to your breathing makes you more anxious, however, move on to the second method, and come back to this one when you feel ready.)

- Settle yourself comfortably in a place where you won't be disturbed. Make sure your clothes are loose.

- Sit or lie comfortably with your hands side by side in your lap, or your arms by your side, and your legs uncrossed.

- Close your eyes.

- Now concentrate on becoming aware of your feet on the floor, your legs and arms where they are resting and your head against the cushion, pillow or chair back.

- Keep your shoulders down and take in a really deep breath – it can be helpful to put your hand on your tummy to feel it inflating like a balloon, as this lets you know that you're doing it right.

- Then make each out-breath last longer than your in-breath. (This is important because the out-breath stimulates the body's natural relaxation response. By changing your pattern of breathing in this way, your body automatically begins to relax.) A good way to do this is to breathe in to the count of 7, then breathe out gently and more slowly to the count of 11. If you cannot breathe out for that long, hold your breath for the remainder of the time while you keep counting to 11 and then breathe in again. Alternatively, try breathing in to the count of 3 and out, more slowly, to the count of 5.

- Do this about 10 to 20 times, knowing that you will relax more with each breath.

- Concentrate on the counting (try not to let your mind wander off; if it does, just gently bring it back) and feel the welcome sense of calm gradually flowing in.

- Try and be aware of how much less tense you feel, just by relaxing your breathing and blocking out your over-busy thoughts.

This 7/11 (or 3/5) technique is good for instant relaxation too. Just do it a few times, wherever you are, if you feel tearful or that a panic attack is coming on or you are getting so wound up that you can't make a simple decision. No one will know you are doing it, so there is no embarrassment to fear.

" A few minutes' calm is a wonderful gift to give yourself. "

2. The clenched fist method

Another good way to relax is through the following simple method, derived from yoga. (However, only use this if you don't have any problems with your hands, such as arthritis.)

- Settle yourself comfortably and then make your hands into the tightest fists possible. (If you have exceptionally long fingernails, just clasp both hands tightly together, interlocking the fingers.)

- Look at your fists carefully as you squeeze them harder and harder, being aware of the whiteness of your knuckles, the feeling of your nails against your palms, the pressure of your thumbs against your forefingers and the rigidity of your wrists. Notice too the tension moving up your arms to your elbows and shoulders.

- Keep squeezing your fists like this and concentrate on the physical sensations for a moment or two. To help you concentrate, close your eyes.

- Then, with all your concentration focused on the change that develops between tension and relaxation, allow your fingers and hands to slowly unwind.

- Still with your eyes closed, feel the enjoyable sensation of relaxation spreading quite naturally through your fingers and up along your arms as the tension drains away. You may find it takes the form of whatever your body needs – coolness if you tend to be too hot or warmth if you tend to feel too cold – or else you might just feel a pleasant tingling sensation.

- Whatever form it takes, let the relaxing sensation spread through your body, relaxing your brow, your cheek muscles, your jaw, your shoulders, chest and so on, down to your toes.

- Keep your focus on the falling away of stress and the calming differences you can sense in your body, perhaps imagining it draining away from your feet and disappearing into the floor.

- You can keep repeating this for as long as you like, while you enjoy noticing the calming changes that occur throughout your body. As your body relaxes, so does your mind.

3. The whole body method

This highly effective method is also derived from yoga and achieves relaxation in a similar way.

- Work gradually through the main muscles of your body, tensing each in turn for a count of 10 and then relaxing them. As in the previous technique, this works on the simple mechanical principle that, if you tense muscles and then relax them, your muscles are always more relaxed afterwards than before you tensed them.

- Try starting with your feet, move up to your calf muscles, then your knees, your thighs, your tummy muscles and so on.*

Create a 'safe and special place'

You can make relaxing an even more pleasant and rewarding experience by using the time with your eyes closed to waft yourself away mentally to some pleasant imaginary place, or to a real place that you love to go to. People often choose to imagine themselves walking on empty beaches by the sea, or in the mountains, or by a stream, or sitting in their own gardens. Children might choose their bedrooms or to imagine themselves in outer space. You can make the scene whatever you want it to be. If you are more relaxed when there are other people around, incorporate their presence into your imaginings too.

Perhaps you relax through a physical activity, such as playing football or squash, dancing, cycling or walking in the park, in which case visualise yourself enjoying that activity. Wherever you choose to be and whatever you choose to do there, concentrate on making the occasion as real as it can be. Really try to *see* the colours of the sandy beach, or the flowers or football shirts. *Hear* the sounds – the gentle whoosh of rippling waves, the rustling of leaves, the voices of the players. *Feel* the textures; *smell* the smells. (You may well find that

---

* A helpful relaxation CD, called *Relax: using your own innate resources to let go of pent-up stress and negative emotion*, is available from the publishers of this book. Call: +44 (0)1323 811662 or order online at: www.hgonline.co.uk As well as relaxing you, using these techniques and others, the CD teaches you about the benefits of relaxation at the same time.

you are 'better' at visualisation than at hearing the sounds or smelling the smells, or better at the sounds or smells than visualisation: this really doesn't matter as we all tend to have one sense that is more dominant than the others; just focus on whatever comes easiest.)

Imagine your chosen scene in detail, so that you can make it your very own 'special, safe place', one you will always be able to call to mind and enjoy when relaxed – or to use to help you to relax, when you need to very quickly.

> 66 Calm yourself down whenever you start becoming overwhelmed with feelings. 99

Deliberately try to calm yourself down in one of these ways, whenever you start becoming overwhelmed with feelings. Just as you can't contract and relax a muscle at the same time, so you can't be anxious when you are in a relaxed state. When you are calm and free from pressing thoughts, even for a short period, you have access to the rational part of your brain and can more clearly recognise and question any black-and-white thinking.

Practise 'mindfulness'

People who suffer from anxiety don't tend to spend much time 'in the moment', absorbed in what they are doing: they are more likely to do things absentmindedly, while they fret about something in the past or worry about the future.

Creating 'mindfulness', a technique for turning off busy thoughts, which derives from Buddhist meditative practices, is a powerful antidote to that. It can be hard to do at first, just because it is so contrary to our usual way of going about things, but perseverance pays. Try it for yourself, by following these simple steps:

- Decide to give your complete attention to a simple task you are familiar and comfortable with. For instance, if you are weeding the garden, be aware of all the movements you make, as you make them, one after another. Be aware of the flowers and weeds you are working with, their textures and colours. Let your focus be *entirely* on the activity you are engaged in and what you are seeing and sensing, but don't *think* about what you are doing.

- If a thought intrudes, whether it concerns what you are doing (for instance, "I'm getting tired", "I'm bored" or "I don't like those flowers") or concerns other matters or worries, just be aware you are having the thought, then gently let it go and bring yourself back to the task in hand. Your aim is to experience, not to think or make judgements or have opinions.

- Whatever your chosen activity, whether it's cooking, eating, dusting, brushing your teeth, changing a tyre, savouring a cup of coffee or anything else, follow the same pattern: be aware of every action you are taking, moment by moment, and the associated textures, colours, sounds and/or smells that you are conscious of as you work.

Taking a little time to practise periods of 'mindfulness' like this will give you a welcome break from the interminable thoughts and worries that fuel anxiety and help to keep your arousal levels down.

Get a good night's sleep

As you will now know from Part 1, getting enough sleep of the right kind is vital for both our health and overcoming anxiety. We need enough slow-wave sleep to restore our bodies and renew our energy, and we need dream sleep to discharge unexpressed emotional arousals from the day, so that we can start tomorrow charged up and ready to go.

But how much sleep is enough? Worrying about not getting enough sleep can actually be a cause of insomnia. Some people, mainly men, can manage quite comfortably on four hours' sleep a night. Others say they have to have 10 hours to feel right. The view from some sleep experts is that most adults don't actually *need* more than seven. But if you wake up refreshed and energised and ready to start the day, you are getting enough sleep, however many

> 66 If you wake up refreshed and energised, you are getting enough sleep ... 99

hours you have had.

It really is important to believe that last sentence, as we will see. In a fascinating study, researchers at Oxford University gave 22 insomniac students a gadget that displayed electronically how much sleep they had had the previous night. But, unbeknownst to the students, the researchers had manipulated the reading. They found that the day after students *thought* they had slept badly (when they had in fact slept quite well) they were more likely to think that they couldn't cope with their

> **"** Insomniacs sleep more than they think they do ... **"**

daily tasks and to suffer physical discomfort, such as feeling sleepy and having tired eyes. It is well known that insomniacs sleep more than they think. So, it is possible that, for you too, anxiety that you *might* not have slept well could be a large cause of any daytime problems you experience.

However, if, instead of waking up feeling refreshed, you feel as though you are a bit drunk or in a daze, can't concentrate properly and forget things, then you are *not* getting enough sleep. So you need to do something about that. Although there are many possible reasons for finding it hard to sleep or for waking early and finding it hard to get back off again (see the panel overleaf), by far the most common is stress. But as well as identifying what is causing the stress and finding ways to reduce it (see next section), it is important to establish good sleeping habits too. This becomes even more crucial as we get older. When we are young, we can sleep anywhere. But, as we age, sleep is a far more fragile state and good sleep patterns must be gently nurtured.

Tips for a better night's sleep

1. It may sound obvious, but *go to bed earlier* if you go to bed very late and always wake up tired!

2. *Avoid drinking tea or coffee late in the evening.*

3. *Avoid drinking too much alcohol.* Having several drinks may indeed get you off to sleep but, in the middle of the

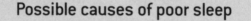

Possible causes of poor sleep

- a pain condition that is not controlled well enough at night

- restless leg syndrome

- sleep apnoea (momentarily ceasing to breathe, every so often)

- eating an evening meal too late

- drinking too much alcohol

- being overstimulated from watching television late at night

- drinking too much caffeine

- exercising too late in the evening

- withdrawing from tranquillisers or alcohol

- jetlag

- depression

- generalised anxiety

- suffering from too much stress

- shift work

night, once the alcohol has been metabolised, your body is in withdrawal and that wakes you up.

4. *Don't take exercise within two hours of bedtime.* But do exercise earlier in the day or evening.

5. *Have a milky drink or camomile tea before bedtime.*

6. *Have a relaxing warm bath or shower before going to bed.*

7. *Ensure you have a comfortable mattress*, not one that is old and saggy.

8. *Put up blackout curtains or blinds*, if necessary, to keep the light from waking you.

9. *Use the bedroom primarily for sleep.* Don't watch television in it or listen to loud music with a fast beat, or do anything else that wires you up. Having sex is good, however – although sex stimulates, it discharges energy and so doesn't adversely affect sleep.

10. *Wear earplugs* if your partner snores, or noise disturbs you from outside.

11. *Make sure you're not too hot or too cold in bed.*

12. *Try spraying some lavender around the bed or use a lavender pillow.* Many people find the scent helps to induce sleep.

13. *Do not nap* at lunchtime or in mid-afternoon.

14. *Don't worry about whether you are sleeping or not!*

And if that doesn't work ...

Two powerful strategies to promote good sleep

1. *Try some visualisation:*

Lie comfortably in your bed and close your eyes. Use one of the methods we described earlier for inducing relaxation and then take yourself off in your imagination to a peaceful, beautiful, quiet place. Perhaps imagine yourself walking by a stream in the cool evening breeze, or strolling along a deserted beach at sunset. While doing that remember times when you've been away somewhere and had the feeling that you've left all your cares behind you. Give yourself the suggestion every so often that, "sooner rather than later, I can drift off into a sound refreshing sleep". This can be a swift, enjoyable way to promote falling into a deep, refreshing sleep.

2. *Unlearn bad habits:*

Sleeping through the night is a conditioned behaviour. It isn't actually natural – indeed, parents have to teach young children to do it! It may be the norm to sleep only at night in cold countries, but in hot countries it is common to take a two-hour sleep during the heat of the day and sleep fewer hours at night. So, our sleep habits are learned. And we can learn bad ones as easily as good ones.

For instance, suppose you watch television till 11 or 12 at night, during which time you fall into a snooze. When you finally get up to go to bed, you are probably wide awake again. You lie there tossing and turning. And the result is that you start to associate bed with being awake instead of asleep. This is called 'reverse conditioning' and we need to undo it.

The important thing is not to reward the brain for staying awake. Some people decide, after lying

> 66 The important thing is not to reward the brain for staying awake ... 99

awake for half an hour, to get up and watch an exciting film or to have something to eat. We even know of people who got into the habit of cooking a mixed grill for themselves every morning at 3 a.m., because they couldn't sleep. But it is imperative that we don't reward the brainstem (the primitive part of the brain that wakes us up) by giving it food or something interesting to do. Instead, it needs to be punished!

And this is how:

- Pick a time to get up each morning and (during this relearning phase) stick to it even on days when you don't have to get up for work or to take the children to school, etc.

- Don't go to bed until you are physically tired.

- If you are not asleep 30 minutes later, get up and do an *extremely boring task*. This must be something (preferably quiet) that you really loathe doing; something you hate doing at any time of day, let alone the night; something you put off and off, or else groan and moan and huff and puff about, whenever you are doing it. It might be working your way through a pile or ironing; doing your accounts; waxing the floor; sewing on buttons or filling before you can decorate. As soon as you are really tired, however, abandon the task and go back to bed.

- If you are still awake 30 minutes later, get up and do another *extremely boring task*. It might be the same one, if you didn't finish before, or it might have to be a different one. If you don't hate any household or work task enough, invent one. Perhaps you must read out loud all the labels on all the jars in a kitchen cupboard. Or get sheets of blank paper and rule 50 lines on each. Be creative about being boring! The brainstem may be primitive and stupid but it's not *that* stupid. If it realises that it is going to get punished instead of getting fed or stimulated, it will very quickly learn to let you sleep through the night.

Celia couldn't sleep

Joe was once contacted by a strong-minded woman in her 50s, called Celia, who said she was desperate to overcome her insomnia. However, she also announced: "But I fear you'll never be able to help me, really. My mother suffers from it, and my grandmother did, and my great-grandmother before that. I'm convinced it's something that runs in the family."

Despite her despondency, Joe relaxed her and began some guided imagery, to try to help her create a pleasant, relaxing place in her mind that she could 'visit' to ready her for sleep. But Celia quickly brought that to a stop, saying "that sort of thing" wasn't 'her' at all.

So Joe moved on to the method just described above. Celia was willing to establish a time to get up each morning and to stay up until physically tired. But, although she was happy to get up again after 30 minutes, if still awake, she balked at carrying out some boring or useless task.

"I don't find any chores boring," she said. "And I get involved in everything I do. I'm certainly not going to waste precious time drawing lines on sheets of paper when I could be using it for reading!"

It turned out that Celia loved reading, although she didn't have as much time to engage in it as she would have liked. Joe decided to make use of that. He suggested that she should choose a book which she would find quite challenging, because of its dense plot or dense writing style. Then, if she was still awake after 30 minutes of trying to sleep, she should get up and read it – standing up.

> **" A week later ... she was sleeping like a baby. "**

She called him a week later to say she was sleeping like a baby.

Find an enjoyable way to unwind

This can be anything that takes you out of yourself. Below are some of the methods used by participants on one of our recent anxiety management seminars:

- playing the piano
- doing yoga
- taking a long, warm, scented bath
- taking exercise to music
- taking a nap
- a long walk with the dog
- reading to children
- cooking
- cleaning or tidying up
- writing

- gardening
- doing crosswords
- going out with friends
- singing
- dancing
- birdwatching
- playing a sport
- watching an engrossing film
- reading an engrossing book

Remember, it is important to make some time for yourself, to do what *you* enjoy doing. This 'down time' is not a luxury. It is an absolute requisite for mental and physical health.

OVERCOMING ANXIETY | 119

Do an 'emotional needs audit' on yourself

Next, it is important to identify what is not going right in your life, so that you can take some practical steps to deal with it. As we have mentioned before, no one suffers from disabling anxiety disorders if their needs are being met in balance and they are making the best use of their innate resources. Therefore, something, somewhere, has gone awry.

So, when you have calmed yourself down and are in a more relaxed state of mind, try to take stock. If you can recall when your anxiety started (whether in the form of generalised anxiety, panic attacks, a phobia or OCD), are you aware of anything that was happening around that time that particularly unsettled you? For instance, did your symptoms start at a time when you were experiencing an upheaval or major change (such as a new job or school, a new home in a new area, a new baby, a break up of a relationship or a bereavement, or perhaps retirement)? Were you anxious about someone's else's wellbeing? Or a crucial exam? Perhaps there was a combination of stressful events? If you can identify such a circumstance, this is useful information for you, as it tells you when your own stress levels reach a pitch that you find difficult to cope with. (A lot of people, however, can't recall anything specific, and it doesn't matter if you can't, either.)

EXERCISE:

We would now like you to turn your attention to what is happening in your life at the moment and to take the emotional
needs audit opposite. As you do so, try to really think about
each question and be as honest and probing as possible. If you
have already identified yourself as a black-or-white thinker,
you might be tempted to say that none of your needs is being
met. But that is unlikely to be true. The very fact that you are
in a position to be concentrating on this book suggests that
something in your life *is* working. Perhaps, as you consider
the following questions, you will find that many things are
working well (or could be), but one big area of dissatisfaction
is overshadowing the rest. Or it could be that certain needs
are getting met but not in the healthiest way for you. The
paragraphs below are intended as a guide, to get you thinking, so, as you work through them, make a note of any areas
that you become aware of in which your needs are not being
satisfactorily met.

Do you feel secure at home, at work and in your environment?

For instance, do you live with someone with whom you have
a loving and caring relationship or with someone you are
fearful of who constantly criticises you – or do you reluctant-
ly live alone? If you are a young person, is your parents' or

How well are your emotional needs being met?

YOU MIGHT like to use this checklist when carrying out your own emotional needs audit. Rate, in your judgement, how well the following emotional needs are being met in your life now, on a scale of one to seven (where 1 means not met at all, and 7 means being very well met).

- Do you feel secure in all major areas of your life? For instance, in your home life, work life or environment?
- Do you feel you receive enough attention?
- Do you think you give other people enough attention?
- Do you feel in control of your life most of the time?
- Do you feel part of the wider community?
- Can you obtain privacy when you need to?
- Do you have at least one close friend?
- Do you have an intimate relationship in your life (i.e. you are totally physically and emotionally accepted for who you are by at least one person)?
- Do you feel an emotional connection to others?
- Do you have a status in life (whatever it may be) that you value and that is acknowledged?
- Are you achieving things in your life that you are proud of?
- Do you feel competent in at least one major area of your life?
- Are you mentally and/or physically stretched in ways which give you a sense of meaning and purpose?

If you have scored any need at 3 or less, this is likely to be a major stressor for you.

Even if you have scored only one need very low, it can be enough of a problem to have a serious, adverse effect on your life, and could well be the cause of your anxiety/stress.

carers' relationship a good one and do you feel secure in your relationship with them? Are you confident at work or school or do you feel undermined or bullied by peers or a boss? Is your work culture authoritarian or inclusive? Is your job secure? Do you dread social occasions where you don't know anyone? If you have a mortgage, can you pay it? Have you been assaulted on the street or burgled at home and are you fearful of it happening again? Do your fears prevent you from doing some things that you would otherwise want to do?

Do you feel you receive enough attention?

And, if so, is it necessarily of the right type? For instance, do you spend most of your time doing things for other people, such as your children, partner or parents, at the expense of your own needs? Do you ever feel that certain other people sap your energy, wanting all your support and a sympathetic ear at any time that suits them, but are prepared to give little back? Are there people who are genuinely interested in what you think and feel? Do you feel appreciated?

Or do you spend a great deal of time alone, whether you want to or because you feel you have no other option? Do you feel too shy to participate much on social occasions or fear them so much that you avoid them altogether? Do you get attention by being anxious and fearful, or by creating scenes and dramas?

Do you think you give other people enough attention?

Do you wholeheartedly spend time doing things with (or for) your friends, children, relatives or needy neighbours? Can you 'hear' what your partner says to you or do you hear only what you expect to? Do you listen to what colleagues have to say? Do you enjoy being the centre of attention, for instance through giving speeches or seminars or presentations or per forming on stage? Do you engage in certain activities just to win attention – for instance, turning to politics or taking up a sport, just to share the interests of the new love in your life? Are you genuinely interested in what others think and do, or just in how their opinions and actions affect you?

Do you feel in control of your life most of the time?

For instance, do you have sufficient responsibility in your work life or too little or too much? Do you have targets or deadlines that you struggle to meet? Can you take the respon-sibility for important decisions in your life? Does someone in your life have too much influence or power over you? Have you recently lost your sense of control, perhaps because of the arrival of a new person at work, a new baby or the introduc-tion into your life of difficult in-laws? Do you feel you should be able to control things that, in fact, you can't – such as how much your children study or how well they do in exams – and blame yourself if things don't turn out as you think they should? Have you developed a physical disability or chronic illness that has taken away a measure of your control? Or perhaps you have debts and other financial worries that you feel you cannot control? Do you feel out of control of your body or your thoughts (resulting in panic attacks or compulsive behaviours?) Maybe you feel left in the dark by others about things that affect you – for instance financial matters or information relating to an illness or treatment?

Do you feel part of the wider community?

Humans are social animals and need social connections. Do you know people outside your close family and circle of friends? Do you help others, such as neighbours, or through voluntary work of any kind? Are you involved with a church or other religious institution? Are you involved with any neighbourhood schemes or local politics or do you participate in any community activities, such as a local drama group, football team, aerobics class or parents' group? Or perhaps you are a school governor or a member of a charity's management committee? Do you have people you say hello to on the street? Have you ceased to participate in regular activities because of a particular changed circumstance, such as loss of a job, a newborn baby or a disability or chronic illness? Have you withdrawn from activities you enjoy because of anxieties, such as fear of a panic attack or the need secretly to perform compulsive activities?

Can you obtain privacy when you need to?

Do you have anywhere in your home that you can withdraw to, to quietly reflect or get on with some task or hobby in peace? Do you have a space that is deemed yours, whether a bedroom or a study or a tree house or a den? Do you feel that your space is constantly invaded by family members? Do you work in an open plan office and, if so, does it offer any measure of privacy, such as screen partitions? Do you feel that your private belongings are respected, and not pried into? Can you/do you take off somewhere alone, if you need to? Are you always available via mobile phone during the day and evening?

Do you have at least one close friend?

That is, is there someone in your life you trust completely and who trusts you, and with whom you are in contact a lot? Do you see them often? Do you do things together? Do you see them less since you or they started a relationship with a new partner? Do you care what they think about you? Do you want the best for them, and do they want the best for you? Could you call on them for help at any time? If you are lonely, do you try to mask it with the anaesthetic of alcohol?

Do you have an intimate relationship in your life?

That is, do you feel totally physically and emotionally accepted for who you are by at least one person. (This could be your
close friend.) Is there at least one per-
son who you know will always be in
your corner, if the going gets tough?
Can you tell them anything? Do they
comfort or advise you, when you are
down, and bolster your confidence,
and enjoy your successes? Do they think you are fun or funny
and a great person to be around? Can you be yourself with
them? Or have you lost the person who meant most to you in
your life? For instance, has a serious relationship recently
ended? Are you grieving for someone who has died?
(Bereavement can make us feel sad and bereft for a long time
but if you are still completely grief-stricken two years after a
loved one's death, that is no longer normal grieving.) Do you
drink – or did you start – to mask the pain of bereavement or
separation? Do you feel fearful that a partner will stray or is
your partner fearful that you might stray? (Sometimes agoraphobia develops in response to accusations of infidelity from
the other partner or as a means of 'keeping an eye on' a partner, because they must stay close by to take over domestic
chores such as shopping, child collection and so on.)

> **66 Really think about
> each question – be
> as honest and probing
> as possible ... 99**

Do you feel an emotional connection to others?

Do you have family and friends you care about a lot, apart from your closest friend? Do you feel cared for by them? Do you speak to or see them often? Or have you lost touch with family or friends or stopped seeing them just lately?

Do you have a 'status' in life that you value and that is acknowledged?

We only know we are accepted by the wider community when we get feedback in the form of acknowledged status. For instance, do your relations, friends, partner, neighbours or colleagues – respect you for the roles you play in life – at work, socially, as a parent or talented musician, knowledge-able gardener etc. – and do you feel valued for how you perform them? Do you feel suitably rewarded or appreciated for what you do? Do at least some people give you high status in at least one area of expertise? Do you feel you should have

achieved more, or that others have done better than you? Do you feel you fit in somewhere, or do you feel an outsider; a non-entity? Do you feel inferior or hostile to others or often

> 66 ... you may find many things are working well in your life. 99

jealous of them? Do you yearn for what you haven't got? Do you feel you have been denied chances in life?

Are you achieving things in your life that you are proud of?

We all need to feel a sense of achievement. For instance, on balance, are you doing what you want to do with your life or have you outgrown or lost interest in what you are doing now? Do you enjoy the way you spend your time and feel satisfyingly stretched by it or do you feel out of your depth? Do you like new challenges? Or do you avoid challenges and stick to what is comfortably familiar, blocking out the thought that perhaps you could achieve more? Do you feel unsatisfied, not challenged, stuck, perhaps because there is nothing further you can achieve at work or your children have grown up and left home? Or are you resting on your laurels – relying on a major past success to feel good about yourself?

Do you feel competent in at least one major area in your life?

When we know we are competent at something, whatever it is, we have evidence that we are not useless. So, do you think you are good at at least some of what you do, whether that is being a parent, holding down a job, managing a career, playing a sport, or using an important life skill such as sewing, gardening, cooking, car maintenance or whatever? Can people rely on your skills? Do people respect your skills? If you don't feel competent, you are likely to have low self-esteem, which comes from a sense of inadequacy and lack of self-belief (see box on page 142–3).

Are you mentally and/or physically stretched in ways that give you a sense of meaning and purpose?

There are three main ways we find meaning and purpose in our lives. First, we all need to feel needed or that we can do something that is of value to others. Are there people in your life who need you? Do you have a caring role as a parent or adult child of elderly parents or within a caring profession? Do you engage in activities that have meaning for others, such as helping out in a charity shop, visiting elderly people, walking a sick person's dog? Secondly, do you have activities that interest and continue to challenge you? (Even if you are retired from work, retirement from life is not an option: you need to stretch yourself and set realistic goals for yourself, whatever age you are.) Thirdly, do you have an overarching philosophy or approach to life that helps you see life as intrinsically meaningful? Do you have a commitment to something bigger than yourself that stretches you, be it spiritual, political, a determination to save the environment or to raise health standards in developing countries?

> 66 We all need to stretch ourselves, whatever our age ... 99

What have you found out?

When you have completed your audit, you may find that your life is working better than you thought, and that your anxiety is blowing a lot of things out of proportion. Or maybe there *are* definite areas of unmet need that could be triggering your anxiety or keeping it going. Or maybe you are meeting some of your needs in unhealthy ways, at the expense of your health or of your relationships with other people. Perhaps your anxiety itself has just become a habit and this habitual anxious response is now stopping you from getting your needs met. It could also be the case that, once you have dealt with a specific problem such as panic attacks or compulsive behaviours, you will have no unmet needs, because the circumstance that triggered them is in the past. If so, it is useful if you have become aware, from the quick 'stock-taking' exercise you did before the audit, of the kinds of stresses that might leave you vulnerable to anxiety in the future. Then you can act promptly to reduce your stress burden or to apply the anti-anxiety techniques you are learning.

Set specific goals for yourself

Once you have identified what it is that is missing in your life, it will be easier to see what you need to start or stop doing, to get your important needs met. Set yourself some clear goals to work towards (these should be small and achievable) and decide on the strategies you will use to achieve them. We will be looking at specific strategies appropriate for different anxiety disorders later.

Be concrete

It is no good deciding that you want to be 'less anxious'. That's too vague. Instead, unpack what 'not being anxious' means to you. Does it mean being able to go to the party instead of turning down the invitation? Does it mean daring to fly in a plane? Does it mean trusting that your grown up children can take care of themselves instead of fruitlessly worrying about them? If you don't find this easy, try putting it this way. "If I woke up in the morning and found that I was no longer anxious, what (realistically) would I be doing that is different from what I do now?"

Be realistic

We cannot turn back the clock and save the leg that has been amputated, or keep the partner who has left, or restore the husband or wife who has died. We cannot make ourselves

younger. Therefore, we must look at our current circumstances and set goals based on those – for instance, to regain
or retain as much fitness as possible, to take up different challenges, to engage in social activities or to meet new people to
spend time with. And, remember, we can feel young, despite
our biological age.

Focus outwards

Most people who are anxious spend a great deal of their time
being self-absorbed, often without realising it. They are wor-

■ MY GOALS	
■ Intention	■ Action

ried about what might happen to *them*, what other people might think of *them*, whether people *they* love will be harmed, how *they* are going to cope, how *they* will find the strength to go on etc. So, a good place to start when making goals is to decide to do something for someone else.

However, if you do a lot of that already, try doing something enjoyable for yourself, without worrying while doing it. Such a goal might be:

- to take a walk and really look at what is around you and be in the moment as much as possible (i.e. enjoy it!)

- to have a conversation with someone, actually listen closely to what they are saying and ask them pertinent questions about what they're telling you

- to invite a friend or friends whom you haven't seen for ages to come to dinner and concentrate on cooking a delicious meal for you all

- to read a chapter of a book that interests you and focus on the words and meaning

- to take up an activity you can really engage in – such as joining a sports club, learning a new skill at a day or evening class, taking up voluntary work, etc. – and be open to getting to know new people there. Even if you suffer panic attacks, you will be able to do such things after you have learned how to handle them. Closing down your life, so that more and more of your innate needs are left unmet, will only exacerbate your symptoms.

Gerry's panic attacks

Ivan once worked with a young man called Gerry who had been off work for eight months because of panic attacks. His symptoms had originally begun when he was experiencing a highly stressful period of major change at work. And a relationship with a longstanding girlfriend had also ended at around the same time. As a result, Gerry gradually started withdrawing from all of the activities he used to enjoy, such as going to the pub with his friends and playing guitar in a small group. Every time he contemplated going back to work or seeing friends in a social setting, he had another panic attack. He was becoming isolated, depressed and now desperate.

It was clear that Gerry felt highly insecure; his attention needs were not being met and he felt out of control most of the time. He had lost his most important, intimate relationship and, through his anxiety, his social and emotional connections had gradually eroded. His status felt uncertain to him, in terms of his work, and he was no longer achieving things or challenging himself. No wonder he felt hopeless. But he wouldn't be able to help himself unless he addressed what was lacking in his life.

Ivan soon found out that Gerry found social situations extremely daunting. He would stumble over his words and blush vividly, unless he was with people he knew well and felt safe with. He could trace all this back to an incident at school when he was 11. His class had been set a poem to learn for homework and, the next day, Gerry was called up in front of them all to recite it. He had learned the poem but, as he looked at the sea of faces watching him expectantly, he suddenly panicked. His heart thumped, his mouth went dry and he couldn't get a word out of his mouth. The teacher drummed his fingers and looked furious. Poor Gerry was left standing there, opening and closing his mouth

> **Unsurprisingly this event had remained live in his emotional memory.**

like a fish, while his classmates started giggling and then openly laughing. Eventually the teacher bawled at him, telling him he was incompetent and a complete disgrace and failure, before sending him to sit down. Unsurprisingly, this event had remained live in Gerry's emotional memory.

When Gerry thought about ringing his boss, he experienced the same sense of incompetence and failure (thinking his boss would criticise him for his long absence). He also panicked at the thought of the questions his colleagues might ask about why he had been off sick so long.

So, to take the emotional arousal out of the memory, Ivan used the rewind technique and then, while Gerry was calm, discussed with him what he *really* thought the reactions of his boss and colleagues would be. (Gerry thought his boss would probably be pleased to hear from him and that his colleagues wouldn't pry if he could make it clear he didn't want to discuss his illness.) Ivan then guided Gerry to visualise himself confidently making the call to his boss, chatting with his colleagues and saying, if anyone asked, "I've been really unwell but I'm fine now". He also encouraged him to visualise himself enjoying an evening out with friends.

Gerry realised that, to get his life back on track, he needed to start making connection with people again, to resume pleasurable group activities and to stop thinking that he would never get another girlfriend. When, a month later, Gerry came to see Ivan again, he had successfully called his boss. He had also returned to work and, to his surprise, no one even asked about why he had been away so long. He had started meeting his friends again and was planning to get back to playing with his group again. What's more the blushing and stumbling over his words had completely stopped, and he now felt positive about the future.

> 66 When he returned a month later, he was back at work, seeing his friends again and feeling positive about the future. 99

Think straight

As we have seen, anxiety is kept alive by negative thinking and worrying. So it is crucial to start challenging this kind of thinking style as soon as possible. Remember, too, that when you stop the ruminating and agonising, you will also sleep better.

First, you need to become aware of all the negative commentary running through your head. You may already be aware of it but a great many people aren't, because it is just an uncon-

> **" Use these tips to help control the negative thoughts running through your head. "**

scious accompaniment to their daily life. Fleeting thoughts such as, "I'm not good enough", "I'll never cope", "I'm a bad person", "It's all my fault", "It's all too much!" are powerful: they suck up our vitality and confidence and take a lot of energy that we could better expend elsewhere. So, here are some useful tips for controlling them.

■ *Try carrying a notebook with you for a few days* ...

And note down every negative thought that you catch coming into your mind. You may well be surprised by just how many there are! Doing this will make you more conscious of negative thinking generally and better able to take the next step.

■ *Challenge the negative thoughts!*

Ask yourself whether they are realistic or whether they represent merely a highly biased view of events. Challenging unrealistic thoughts will help disempower them and push them out of your mind – altogether.

"I'm not good enough."

"Actually, I'm doing my best in very difficult circumstances."

"I'm always late!"

"Occasionally I'm late."

"I'll never cope."

"I've always managed to cope so far, one way or another."

"I'm a bad person."

"I love my children and my husband, and I do my best for them."

"It's all my fault."

"It's partly my fault and partly his/hers."
"It was actually completely unavoidable."

"It's all too much!"

"If I can't do it all, I'll just do what I can."
"I'll do 7/11 breathing for a few moments and see how I feel about it then."

"I'll die if I don't get invited!"

"I'll be disappointed if I don't get an invite, but there will be others."

"My essays have to be perfect before I can hand it in – can't they see that's why I keep missing the deadlines."

"It's better to make my essay as good as I can get them, and hand them in on time, than hang on to them and get no marks at all!"

"It can never be perfect. It just has to be good enough."

"I might fail. So I won't do any work, then at least I won't be surprised or disappointed by failure."

"I shall try my best. I might even get a very good mark. If I don't, I'll never know what I have to improve to get better marks next time."

■ *What can you do about it now?*

Over-anxious people often spend a lot of time imagining terrifying future events, such as car crashes in which loved ones die, hitherto unknown strains of flu that wipe out their entire family or holidays going disastrously wrong. Or they worry incessantly about past failures and how they might have acted better in a relationship or a work situation or whatever. If that sounds like you, it is helpful to ask yourself, "What can I actually do about it *now*?" If there *is* something you can do (ensuring the car is well serviced, for instance, or taking out holiday insurance), make a note to do it – and then *do* it. If there is nothing you could possibly do to prevent a particular eventuality or to change what has happened in the past, however, then resolve to stop worrying about it.

■ Say "Stop!"

If a particular worry keeps coming into your mind, sometimes just saying "Stop!" very loudly to yourself, inside your head, is enough to prevent it from having house room for a while.

■ Have a worry half hour

Agree with yourself that you will put all of your worries aside until a specific half hour in the day – a time that suits you best but not just before bedtime – when you will sit and do nothing but worry. So, when worries flash into your mind at other times, either note them down to worry about later or, if you know you'll remember them because they are old favourites, just push them away till the appointed time. People often find it much easier to block out intrusive worries when they know they can give them their full attention later. Then, when your worry half hour arrives, you can either worry pointlessly for the whole half hour or, if there are steps you could take to deal with your concerns, you might like to use the time to work on those instead. If you don't feel like worrying for a full 30 minutes, stop short of the time. But remember that is your allowance used up for the day and you don't get to 'make the time up' on any other day!

■ *Exaggerate*

This might sound strange, but exaggerating can really help to put things in perspective. When Ivan has sensed it would be appropriate, he has sometimes told anxious worriers, coming to him for therapy, that they were simply not worrying enough! He then lists dozens and dozens more things they could worry about, piling them up into a huge mountain of absurd, catastrophic scenarios. This soon becomes so ridiculous that his clients collapse with laughter, sometimes even joining in the game.

In one such case, a young film script writer had become obsessed with how easy it is for people to kill another person. *"Every house has knives in!" "Cars are everywhere!"* He couldn't get such thoughts out of his head and was now worrying that this might mean *he* was going to kill somebody. A creative, intelligent man, he had a great sense of humour but was spending 15 hours a day working on his own, writing and researching. So, although he was intellectually stretching himself, his other emotional needs were being neglected. Ivan decided to used the exaggerating technique on him. As their conversation developed, he began suggesting to the writer, as if in all seriousness, all the countless crazy ways people could kill one another with ordinary objects. It soon

> 66 Once put into perspective the sinister obsession never came back. 99

became farcical. His client kept trying to go one better in absurdity until they were both in tears of laughter. Once put into perspective, the sinister obsession never came back. The writer began rebalancing his life, taking into account all his other needs, and his anxiety levels dropped away.

Low self-esteem

SOME ANXIOUS people can come to think that they are rubbish ... and they are then described as having 'low self-esteem'. They feel inadequate, not good enough, not clever enough, not competent enough in some area or other. It could be that, when they were young, they were told they were unlovable, worthless, bad, unwanted or stupid, and they took in those false messages and were conditioned by them to think they were true. But it doesn't always come about like that. Because of a tendency to overreact to negative events, like losing a job or a lover, some people will catastrophise these types of situation to such an extent that they write themselves off as worthless beings.

Self-esteem is a buzz term with psychologists and self-help experts – 'having it' is seen as vital for mental health – but it isn't something you can get by standing in front of the mirror and telling yourself you are a wonderful, lovable person, as some self-help approaches recommend. Feeling good about yourself emerges naturally when you engage with life in a meaningful way. When you master new skills and develop new competencies and feel sure of the support of good friends and the love of ▶

Take a different perspective

If you tend towards black-and-white thinking, you may believe that there are only two possibilities in any given situation (it's great or it's terrible; it's working or it isn't; it's right or it's wrong). But this is primitive, emotional thinking which you fall into because anxiety keeps you emotionally aroused. And, as we have mentioned before, when you are emotionally aroused, you don't have full access to your rational mind and all the possible subtleties of thought. This

> people close to you, self-esteem is yours. When we participate in activities that truly have value to us, and when we are helping and serving others, that is when we feel best about who we are. This is a very good reason for working to break the pattern of negative thinking that might be locking you into low self-esteem as well as anxiety.
>
> **High self-esteem**, incidentally, is not the opposite of low self-esteem, and it is not something to strive for. People with high self-esteem tend to be selfish and greedy, and take little account of other people's feelings and opinions.
>
> **Self-esteem goes up and down** according to how things are working for you. We are more effective at some times than others, just as we can concentrate better at some times rather than others. When self-esteem drops, therefore, it is a signal that something needs addressing in your life.

is why you need to work actively to keep yourself calm.

Then, when you are calm, you can let yourself see the bigger picture, the more optimistic outcome, the creative solution. Taking a more positive, empowering perspective on events in this way is what therapists term 'reframing'. A good therapist will do this quite naturally – and sometimes we do need another, perceptive person to help us see what we were blind to before. But you can also reframe for yourself and learn to make it second nature too. Reframing opens up entirely new possibilities to try out and allows you to explore options instead of rigidly sticking within your own narrow interpretation of events. When you are stuck, reframing can help unstick you.

EXERCISE:

Reframing is, in effect, a refinement of challenging negative thoughts. So, when you think something negative about yourself or someone else, try, as an exercise, to come up with a few alternative viewpoints. The aim is not to explain away problems or to avoid taking responsibility for certain attitudes or actions but to generate new thoughts that open up possibilities rather than close them down, and that consequently may help you to move forward. For instance:

"Why do I always go and say yes when friends ask to stay the weekend? It is so much work and I get so stressed."

"It takes me out of myself when people stay and we laugh and have a good time. Perhaps we could get a takeaway instead of me having to cook."

"When my boyfriend corrects me, he is showing his contempt for me."

"When my boyfriend corrects me, he is just trying to be helpful."

"My boyfriend can't stop himself correcting me. He just has to have things right."

"I was an unwanted child."

"I know what it is like to be unwanted, so it means a great deal to me to know that my partner and my friends have all positively chosen me, and that I matter to them."

"Even though my mother was just 17 when she had me and wasn't ready to cope with being a mother, there were plenty of people who gave me love and care and attention in my childhood."

"I find it hard to say no."

"I'm not a selfish person."

"I like to be helpful."

"Nothing is ever done well enough for my liking."

"I can really appreciate the effort that has gone into this."

"I should do more exercise."

"I'll find a way to make exercise fun, and then I'll want to do it."

Reframing fear of childbirth

Some women are extremely anxious about the prospect of giving birth for the first time. This is not surprising, as friends or relatives may have given them chapter and verse of their own extremely painful/protracted or complicated deliveries. Or, if they have been spared that, they may have been scared to death by dramatic depictions of difficult births in films and TV hospital dramas, where the whole process may be accompanied by much screaming and writhing, with nurses and doctors in a desperate race against time to deliver the at-risk baby.

Some women may, of course, be fearful because they have undergone a previous, highly traumatic birth for real. If that is the case for you, the rewind detraumatisation technique (described in Part 3) can resolve this fear.

If you are pregnant for the first time and fearful of childbirth – or so fearful that you daren't even get pregnant – relax yourself by one of the methods described earlier and then read these words:

"This may be your first time having a baby but the part of your brain that is going to be in charge of giving birth to your baby has done it thousands of times. Because it was passed on to you by your mother, who could only have given it to you if she had successfully given birth to you. And her mother passed it to her and her mother's mother before that and so on,

right back to the beginning of mammalian life on this planet,
300 million years ago. In all that time, that programme hasn't
failed once, or you wouldn't be here. You may be unsure of
what to do or what to expect, but your unconscious mind
knows all about it."

We have said something along these lines to many clients
over the years and they have found it enormously reassuring.

Reframing fear of dying

Naturally enough we fear dying because it is an unknown
experience. And the unknown always raises anxiety. But a
deep fear of dying, even when young and well, is only likely
to arise because other needs are not being met, and these
need addressing.

For many elderly and terminally ill people, their fear of
dying can increase not only because death is relentlessly
approaching but also because dying is so often pushed into
the background. It is relegated to the side rooms in hospitals,
talked about in hushed voices – or not discussed at all – so
people's anxieties are not addressed. However hard it is for
you, therefore, try to discuss it, if they want to. Dying is
something we must all do, after all. However, it is often fear
of pain, rather than fear of dying, which is paramount.
Fortunately modern drugs can usually minimise any physical pain involved.

Sometimes it is appropriate to distract people from their fear of dying. Splitting their attention minimises the fear. Get them to focus on whatever else you can: interesting happenings in the family or the wider world, happy memories, past achievements, other people's lives, humorous or curious stories. Laughter is a tranquilliser with no side effects, so make them smile and laugh. If there is a practical problem they are worrying about, perhaps about who will look after their spouse or how their bills will be paid, demonstrate to them that they can be solved, by you or somebody else, so they don't have to worry about it any more. If they have any regrets about things they did or did not do in life, reframe this as part of the human condition. We all have such regrets but wallowing in them is a great waste of time and energy – we all end up having to let everything in this world go eventually, including all those we love. They may like to speculate about 'life after death'. If so, try to join them in such talk in a thoughtful and comforting way. Never scoff. Whatever your own beliefs remember that the vast majority of people in all cultures and at all times have taken comfort and meaning from feeling themselves connected to a greater, eternal, reality.

For some people, the focus of the fear is not dying but being dead. There are two ways to look at this.

> 66 Laughter is a tranquilliser with no side effects ... 99

Do you (or the person concerned) believe in life after death? If not, there is no point in worrying about how people are getting on in your absence or what is happening to your decomposing body – because you won't have any knowledge of it. It won't matter. If a dying person is concerned about how loved ones will cope without them, the best way to allay the fear is, as mentioned above, to carry out some planning – decide what to leave to whom, arrange who will take care of whom, ensure the will is up to date, etc. If the concern is about being forgotten, it can be helpful to create a memory book or plan the content of a memorial service. Ivan's father, for example, spent a little time each day during the three years before he died, at the age of 95, writing memories of his life, even though it was a struggle and his eyesight by that time was very poor. The resulting memoir is now a much-loved family heirloom.

However, if a person believes in life after death, this opens up options for reframing. Death can be compared to birth. In the womb, we felt totally secure and all of our needs were met. Yet, when the time was right, we were ready to move on, into another world, the one we live in now. We had no idea what this realm would be like but we had the courage to come here, releasing the hormone that triggered

> **66** Allay the fear of how others will cope without them by carrying out some planning … **99**

our own birth process. Death, too, is like that. It is the entering of another, unknown realm and crossing a threshold into another level of being. People who have near-death experiences often sense themselves in a tunnel with light and a welcoming presence at the end, and are at first disappointed to 'return' to life, when they realise their 'time' hasn't come. But after the experience, they commonly cease to fear death and become less materialistic. Death, they feel assured, is not an end but another beginning.

In such ways, one can think more creatively and reassuringly about natural life processes.

Nothing is as certain as change

The one certainty in life, apart from death, is that circumstances *always* change. Of course, that is often what makes people anxious, as they can't rely on things staying the same. The company we work for may be taken over; our children may take to drugs; global warming may change the planet; there could be major war. But we can also turn the fact that things change to our advantage. It means that setbacks can be seen as temporary instead of permanent. Good times will follow bad and, when bad things happen again (as they will), we know they will not last.

There is a wonderfully simple means for creating the expectation of positive change. All you do is use words and phrases that put a time limit on whatever undesirable set of circumstances are in place right now. For instance, instead of thinking, "I'll never have a relationship that works!", try "I haven't met the right person *yet*." The difference in emphasis is life-changing. In the first thought, no possibility is allowed that a future relationship might be different; every relationship will fail. In the second thought, there is a clear expectation that it is possible to meet a person with whom a happy relationship can be developed. The door is closed only on the past, unhappy ones.

EXERCISE:

Consider the following and then try coming up with some for yourself, whenever a negative old favourite pops into mind.

"I get anxious in supermarkets."
"*Till now*, I've been anxious in supermarkets."

"All my relationships fail."
"My *previous* relationships were unsatisfactory."

"I wish I could give up smoking but I never can."
"I've *reached the point* where I want to give up smoking."

"I'll never get over his going off with another woman.
"I'm really hurting *at the moment*."

"There's no way out."
"I haven't found the best way of dealing with this *yet*."

These are not word tricks. They actually refocus the brain *away* from the unrealistic emotional thoughts that shackle you and prevent you from seeing opportunities for creative problem solving.

Set the record straight

A common cry from children is "It's just not fair!" They have a strong sense of injustice and may feel incensed if a teacher wrongly accuses them of being the one to have yelled out in class, thrown a paper dart or started a fight. If they don't feel able to speak up or their protests are rejected, they may come to feel badly about themselves. If they are persistently over-ruled or cannot shake off a reputation as a troublemaker that they perceive as unjust, they may learn a sense of helplessness or passivity that persists into adulthood. As adults, too, being wrongly accused or unfairly put down can sap our confid-ence and reduce our trust in others.

So it is useful to develop the habit of setting the record straight whenever possible, if unwarranted criticisms or angry remarks are made to you. For instance, without thinking, a boss might fume, "Oh, haven't you even finished that piece of work yet?" (Subtext: "You are so slow.") Instead of squirming in silence and feeling put down, try speaking up, not to excuse but to explain: "I had to stop to deal with such-and-such a crisis, but I'm nearly there now".

It doesn't matter whether your explanation is accepted or even acknowledged. By standing up firmly for yourself, but without being rude, you can't help but feel better about yourself.

Have a good laugh

Anxious people very often take themselves and their dilemmas too seriously. Having a good laugh is not only a great way to lighten up, but also an excellent way of reducing stress. And it is, in effect, a whole-body workout. It gets your heart and lungs functioning at full tilt and relaxes the diaphragm, which, when you're anxious, spends a lot of time being hard and tense.

■ *Get yourself a joke book*

As well as getting you laughing for a moment, good jokes help break through black-and-white thinking, and open you up to different expectations. When you hear or read a funny story or a joke, you are already expecting the unexpected: a development you hadn't anticipated or a clever punch line. Momentarily, at least, you have shifted your mindset.

■ *"A funny thing happened ..."*

Remind yourself of 10 things that recently made you laugh or

10 of the funniest things that ever happened to you. Note them down, so that you can look at them to break the spell if you get into a trance of anxious thinking at a later date. Remembering funny experiences from the past is especially salutary because, very often, they weren't the least bit funny at the time. Maybe you locked yourself out of your home with no money or no clothes on. Or the washing machine had a seizure and the kitchen floor was flooded just when a prospective buyer came to view the house. It is a good reminder that even apparent catastrophes aren't as overwhelming as they seem at the time – they can even be laughed about and savoured when put into perspective. And even if you don't find an anxious episode funny as yet, try running it through your mind in a form where the main characters (for instance the angry boss, the domineering mother-in-law) are cartoon or caricature versions of themselves. Or try that other well-tested method of taking the negative power out of a bad memory of over-controlling individuals – imagine the main players naked.

> 66 It is a good reminder that catastrophes aren't as overwhelming as they seem at the time ... 99

■ *Laugh five times a day*

Apparently, on average, happy children laugh over 300 times a day but adults less than 20. So, set yourself the pleasant task of laughing *at least* five times a day. If you have been gloomy and morose, find your list of funny things and see if you can get a laugh out of them. Or deliberately recall times when you cried with laughter – chances are that that alone will set off your funny bone again! Alternatively, try watching a daft film or reading a book that makes you laugh. Or go for a walk and keep an eye out for something that will at least make you smile – the antics of dogs playing in the park, for instance, or something a young child says (such as the exchange a colleague of ours once had: "Are you Jack's mother?" "Yes" answered our colleague. "Oh!" said the little girl, her face brightening, "Do you know his brother Billy?") Again, the benefits exceed the amusement you may enjoy: looking out for everyday examples of the funnier side of life will keep you focused outward for a while, instead of inward.

A young princess had inexplicably lost the power to speak. She languished in her bed chamber, pale and distraught and barely able to eat. None of the court doctors could find what was wrong with her and the king and queen were at their wits' end. But one day she caught sight, from her window, of a young country fellow struggling down the road with a donkey on his shoulder. Now it turns out that this young lad was a bit of a simpleton. He had recently started his first job as a farmhand but had dropped the coins he was given as his day's wages. As a result his irate mother had told him he should have put them in his pocket. So, the next day, when he was given a vessel containing milk for his labours, he poured the milk in his pocket. "Ridiculous boy! You should have carried the vessel on your head!" screamed his mother. The next day, he was rewarded with cream cheese and duly put it on his head - and so on and so on, until the day after he had dragged a ham along the ground on a string and was told he should have hoisted it on to his shoulder. This next day, he had been given a donkey. When the princess saw the poor donkey braying and struggling and the young fellow staggering and scolding, the whole scene was so ludicrous that she burst out laughing. And her paralysing trance state was broken ...

Remind yourself of what you've got going for you

If your instant response to the above suggestion is "Nothing", you are in the grip of black-and-white thinking. So take some deep relaxing breaths and think again.

We all have an enormous number of resources available to us, and by that we mean the skills, experiences and attributes we have developed and accumulated to date, which we can call on at any time to help us navigate our way through life. We may take some of them for granted or forget them or even deny them, however, if we are in a state of negative thinking.

> 66 We all have an enormous amount of resources available to us ... 99

Perhaps you are out of a job and you don't have a relationship at the moment. It is important, then, to remind yourself of the jobs you have successfully held in the past, the qualifications you may have gained, the skills you have learned which enable you to do those jobs, and so forth. Count it as a resource that you have had boyfriends or girlfriends in the past and are therefore capable of making a relationship work; or that you were married for many years before your marriage broke down, and that during most of that time you were a loving, caring partner, capable of sharing and having fun and being fun to be around.

If you have ever carried out responsibilities in your life, whether in a job or at home or even when doing a paper round in your youth (getting up early and going out on dark, cold, wet mornings is no mean achievement), count it as an important resource. It means you have what it takes to hold down or discharge responsibilities effectively again.

If you have loved anyone in your life – your parents or your siblings, if not a life partner – or have cared for people in a professional capacity, you can count on having loving feelings and being able to love and care for others.

If you have just one exam pass to your name, that still shows you had the ability to follow through and complete a course of work in that subject, to turn up for the exam and to keep your nerve for long enough to take and pass it.

Perhaps you are great at drawing cartoons or animals for your nephews and nieces to colour in. Or you knit scarves to give to charity shops. Or you read your children stories at night and give all the characters voices.

Count as a resource even adversities you have weathered. Perhaps you have had years of illness that you have had to cope with or you have survived an acrimonious divorce or you have managed not to go under, despite financial losses. These are huge resources.

Don't forget aspects of your character either. Perhaps people feel you are a sympathetic listener. Or you are kind to stray dogs. Or you have a great sense of humour.

EXERCISE:

Write a list of everything you've got going for you. Be thorough. No skill is too small. Reminding yourself of your resources will help you to access them more easily, build your confidence and think more positively and productively about the future.

Uncouple unhelpful pattern matches

If you spend a lot of time in a state of anxiety, your amygdala (that tiny structure in the brain that acts as an alarm system) is working overtime. The more hyper-aroused you are about all sorts of things, the more it registers them as life-threatening events and sets the panic button off whenever it thinks that something similar is happening again.

But, as we know, the amygdala is not a sophisticated organ. It often does the equivalent of 'cry wolf' but you never get to know that. You behave as though it is a real wolf every time – and, to your emotional brain, it is. But you also have access to the higher brain power of the rational mind, so it is important you use it to supply the amygdala with better information.

> **"** ... calm yourself down and see if you can identify the pattern match ... **"**

This means that, if you find yourself beginning to react in a panicky way that is completely out of proportion to the situation you are in, immediately set about calming yourself down with 7/11 breathing and see if you can identify what your amygdala might be pattern matching to. Perhaps you are on a train and suddenly you feel an inexplicable need to get off it. Why? Is it, perhaps, because three new passengers have just got on and, by chance, one of them looks somewhat similar to a former employer who used to bully you? If you are able to calm yourself in time, you may be able to focus on the fact that this is *not* the same person, that they are not even paying you the remotest attention and that they intend you no harm. You might remind yourself too that the abusive relationship is in the past and cannot inflict further harm on you either. You are perfectly safe on the train and have no need to panic.

It isn't always possible to identify pattern matches because, when they arise from a highly traumatic experience, elements of the pattern match may be unconscious, as described earlier. In such cases, detraumatisation through the rewind technique can deal with the problem.

Commonly, many anxious people pattern match to failure. So, when a new challenge must be faced, if anything remotely similar was ever attempted unsuccessfully in the past, that is what the amygdala will latch onto. This is another good reason for listing your resources. There will no doubt be many forgotten occasions when you faced challenging situations successfully, and recalling these will bring them to the fore and make them more likely to become positive pattern matches in future. Other ways to achieve the same effect are to challenge negative thinking, as described earlier, and rehearse success through visualisation (see page 107).

Rate how you are feeling

Extreme anxiety can, as explained, be caused by misuse of the imagination – by catastrophising and imagining awful futures for ourselves. So it goes with the territory, then, that we will often think things are worse than they are – or remember them as worse than they were. A good way to counter this and get a more realistic picture of how we are doing and coping is to scale how anxious we feel *immediately after doing something we would normally find anxiety-provoking*. It has to be done straight away or negative emotional recall will kick in!

Try carrying a small notebook around with you – it could be the same one you might be using for recording negative thoughts. Draw a line across a page and put a figure 1 at the left end, representing 'really terrible' and a figure 10 at the right end, representing 'really good'. If you tend to wake up anxious, scale yourself first thing in the morning. Maybe it will be a '1'. But then see how it goes through the day. How do you feel when you set off for work? How do you feel when preparing to go into a meeting/attending an interview with your child's teacher/going into a shop/rushing to catch a train? How do you feel when you get home after a busy day? How do you feel an hour before bedtime?

If you do this every day for a few weeks, you will soon see

whether certain activities make you more anxious than others or whether it is particular occasions or places that do so. You will also see how far practising your 7/11 breathing, countering negative thoughts and other self-help suggestions made so far, reduce your anxiety levels. If you have the proof before your eyes, you will have the motivation to continue.

Or maybe the levels aren't falling yet. Is this because of a particular concern that actually needs tackling, rather than worrying about? Or because you are forgetting to apply the techniques? This is all useful information.

Some people like to scale at set times throughout the day and note down what they were doing at the time, so that they can build up a realistic picture of how anxious they really do feel in a 24-hour period. Sometimes we forget all the things that we enjoy or feel on top of because the anxiety is so overwhelming and unpleasant when it does kick in. Some people, therefore, deliberately scale their anxiety levels after pleasant activities – both to remind themselves of the times that they don't feel anxious or to see if they are spoiling even pleasure by worrying.

And don't be black and white in terms of what you think is a satisfactory improvement. Of course, it will be terrific if you reliably start shifting from a '3' to a '7'. But what if you just go from a '1' on one day to a '2' the next. It doesn't seem much, yet it actually represents a 100 per cent increase in anxiety control! If, in a week, you double that, to a '4', and then in three weeks double it again to an '8', you have still soared from your lowest point to an '8' in just a month! This could be quite an achievement if you have suffered disabling anxiety for years.

Be prepared, though, to slide up and down the scale at certain times. This isn't relapse, however. It is a natural process which provides you with useful information you can learn from. For example, what specifically was happening that made anxiety soar at a particular point? Was it a situation, a person, or a thought? And what techniques could you make a point of applying to help counter that?

Separate yourself from your anxiety

Inappropriate anxiety is *not* an intrinsic part of you, although it probably feels that way if you describe yourself as an 'anxious person'. But **you are not your anxiety**. Like every other baby, you came into the world wide-eyed and curious, not a 'neurotic mess', as you may feel now. Think of times when you have been relaxed or had fun or been engrossed in a film or a book (there will be something of the kind you can recall!) Anxiety wasn't in the picture then. Anxiety is either a feeling that suddenly envelops us or, on other occasions, insidiously creeps over us without our realising. It is not the essence of who we are. It

> **66** Remember: you are not your anxiety. **99**

takes us over and, if we can calm ourselves down, it goes away again. If anxiety feels as if it is there all the time, it is because our stress levels have become so high that they have submerged our memories of better times.

But it wasn't always like that, if you can relax enough to think back over your life. At some point, you were not always anxious. (Some people who were abused in early childhood, perhaps, or brought up in a war zone, may not be able to recall a period before anxiety. However, as we have said, such feelings of hyper-anxiety created by post-traumatic stress can be resolved through the rewind technique.) It is, therefore, far more helpful to think of unproductive anxiety as an unwanted visitor. Look at it as something outside yourself and be curious as to why it has bubbled up right now.

When you do this, you are using the rational part of your brain – your 'observing self'. You can recognise it for what it is and more easily decide how to respond, instead of getting emotional and letting anxiety take you over. Remember, anxiety should serve *you* – whenever you need that little edge to get you ready to run a race, make an important speech, or dive in the deep end – but you don't ever have to serve *it*. Unproductive anxiety is, by its very nature, an utter-

> **Anxiety should serve you – you shouldn't serve it. Once it has alerted you, you don't need it anymore.**

ly superfluous emotion. Remember, once it has alerted you, you don't need it. Once the letter has been delivered, the postman doesn't hang around.

We often suggest that people give their anxiety a 'form'. If you had to describe it as in the shape of something, what might it be? For one person it might be like a buzzing insect, a pest that they need to bat away. Another might see it as a straitjacket that they need to wrestle out of. Other people we have worked with have decided, "It's a black blob" (to be dissolved) or "It's a pink jelly" (to be devoured and thus rendered harmless). Someone else settled on a black cloud that could be blown away; another one saw it as a jack-in-a-box, which she put a heavy weight on. Not everyone works best with a visual image. Some people may choose a jarring sound, which they can choose to turn off, or a bad smell that they can kill with a pleasant one.

EXERCISE:

Give this some careful thought, so that you can come up with an image or sensation that has power for you and that you can actively turn off, disable, eliminate, brush away or whatever is appropriate, at will.

Use the *positive* power of your imagination

It is impossible to be in the grip of anxiety unless you are running a fantasy through your brain that is terrifying the life out of you! This is strong evidence indeed of just how powerful our imagination is. In fact, it is so powerful that just imagining something you are nervous about doing or running pictures through your mind of a past frightening event is sufficient to switch on the fight-or-flight response (just as reliably as if we had in reality come face to face with a pack of hungry hyenas whilst walking across the plains of Africa). But, again, this is pure *misuse* of imagination, which evolved to help us find both practical and creative solutions to problems. So instead we need to be firmly determined to take control of the switch and to use our imagination as an anxiety-reduction tool instead of an anxiety-production one.

We all use our imagination all of the time, even if we don't think of ourselves as imaginative people. For instance, if we need a new sofa and like the look of one we see in a shop, we don't buy it just because it is attractive or a nice colour or the right price: first of all, we imagine how it will look in *our* living room. We don't have difficulty creating an image or a sense of our living room in our heads and it is real enough to enable us to judge whether this new sofa will look too large, and dominate the room, or set it off perfectly. Or whether its colour will go with the colours we've already got or clash horribly. Our imagination helps us make the right decision. As an everyday example, if we need to store a number of small items, we *imagine* a suitable receptacle and then go off and find one. Even in these small ways, our imagination is always working.

But it is also far more powerful than that. Imagination enables us to look back to what worked in the past and apply that solution, with perhaps some appropriate modifications, to a challenge we are facing in the future. Just as pilots first learn to fly by working the controls in a simulator, before they try out in a real plane, so we can try out options or rehearse probable outcomes in our imagination before testing them out for real. That's why we like to call the imagination our 'reality simulator'.

EXERCISE: Give your own 'reality simulator' a try

The technique we are going to describe next is one that effective therapists use a great deal to help people establish new, empowering expectations in the place of negative fantasies. We call it 'mental rehearsal'.

First, find a quiet place at a time you won't be disturbed and relax yourself, using the method you like best from the ones we described earlier (see page 102).

Decide on an anxiety-provoking situation that you want to

try out a new response to. You might, for instance, be about to take your driving test soon, an anxiety-provoking event indeed. However, don't bring to mind, in glorious techni-colour and with full soundtrack, all those past occasions when the car slid backwards while you were attempting a hill start or when you reversed around the corner and half way across the road (as this is all sure to get your heart racing unhelpfully). Instead, vividly see yourself driving calmly and confidently to the test centre with your instructor or compan-ion, greeting the examiner with a firm handshake, calmly answering his or her initial questions, confidently opening the car door, being calm and alert as you start the engine and so forth. See yourself carrying out the required manoeuvres successfully, drawing on your real-life experience of having done so many times in the past. Tell yourself, "I can do this."

If you carry out this procedure several times on different occasions before the day, you are doing something very astute. You are harnessing the power of expectation. For, as we explained in Part 1, once an expectation is set up, the brain wants to carry it out. Just as surely as you have sometimes previously brought on disaster by fantasising catastrophes, so you can hugely enhance your likeli-hood of success by creating the expectation you will succeed.

> " ... using your 'reality simulator' in this way will hugely enhance your likelihood of success. "

Using your reality simulator in this way, whenever you are facing a challenge, is both a highly pleasant and effective means of undoing unhelpful pattern matches. But it isn't magic. No amount of imagining will help you pass your driving test if you haven't done enough real practice. Nor, of course, will it bring success in any other area where you haven't done the necessary preparation: you can't give a talk about life in Mongolia unless you know the subject. What it will do, however, is help prevent disabling anxiety from sabotaging all the preparation and practice that you *have* done.

Try to live more healthily

Getting sufficient exercise and eating healthily both have a positive effect on the mind as well as the body.

When you are in a continual state of anxiety, your body is doing the equivalent of getting all dressed up with nowhere to go. The energy the stress hormones create doesn't get properly discharged. Giving your body some kind of work out (sufficient to induce a bit of puff and sweat) will help to get those trapped stress hormones out of your system. Make sure it is something you find enjoyable. You don't want exercising to become yet another 'should' that brings guilt when you don't do it. If it is fun, you will want to do it. A brisk walk with a friend might suit you. Or a regular game of badminton or squash. Or maybe a morning swim with someone you know and bagels for a breakfast treat together afterwards. It's almost impossible to feel anxious after a good swim. Whatever appeals, those are the things to go for. We have suggested, if you notice, activities you might do with someone else. Paying attention to what someone else is doing as well as yourself is more likely to keep you from any habitual negative introspection. However, if you really love to walk or run or jog alone, by all means do it; just try to stay 'in the moment' or to use the time to problem solve productively.

You also want to be sure to have a good, healthy diet, with regular meals, not snatched sugar- and fat-laden snacks. If you have a busy, stressful lifestyle, proper meals, for yourself at least, can often be the first essential that falls by the wayside. You don't have to be a cordon-bleu cook but you do need to eat what your body and mind require to function at their best.

> ❝ The occasional setback doesn't mean you are back to square one – far from it. ❞

Wholegrain cereals, bread, pasta, rice and other whole foods such as lentils, beans and nuts, should be on the menu, if possible. And aim for the now famous five or more daily servings of fruit and vegetables per day. Protein is important: it can be found in eggs, preferably free range and organic, and/or lean meats; and fish such as herring, mackerel, salmon or sardines, which contain the omega-3 oils highly important for brain function.

OVERCOMING ANXIETY | 171

(Because some fish may be polluted, pregnant women are often advised to take omega-3 supplements instead.) It is also a good idea to monitor your sugar intake: too much can itself cause anxiety reactions. And be aware that coffee, tea, alcohol and cigarettes can all trigger production of stress hormones.

Watch for warning signs

Changing the habits of what may have been almost a lifetime is quite a challenge. So don't be surprised or discouraged if you have the occasional setback when a panic overwhelms you or your mind is just a fug. It doesn't mean that you are back to square one: far from it.

Setbacks are learning experiences. As soon as you are able to bring your new skills to bear, calm yourself down and consider, from your 'observing self' what might have brought it on. Perhaps you were tired and run down and not able to access your coping skills. Perhaps you pattern matched to a past powerful negative experience without even realising it. Remember, your nervous system has been hyper-aroused for quite a time, and so it is really no surprise if occasionally it flares up in reaction to some quite minor stress.

Try to become alert to signs that might indicate that you are becoming over-anxious. These might include:

- difficulty concentrating
- difficulty falling asleep

- restlessness
- irritability
- suffering headaches
- feeling tense
- feeling faint
- withdrawing from enjoyed activities
- smoking or drinking more
- sweating.

If you become aware of any, or a cluster, of these symptoms, it could be a reaction to a new, stressful circumstance. Or maybe you have stopped applying your anxiety-reduction skills. Whichever it is, don't panic! Look over Part 2 of this book again and put your skills back into practice.

Coping with panic attacks, agoraphobia and social phobias – special advice

You will now know, if you have read Part 1, that the physiological symptoms of panic can be explained very simply and that it is your interpretation of those symptoms ("I'm having a heart attack!" "I can't cope!" "I'm going to die") that cause them to escalate unbearably. But just knowing that isn't always enough to enable us to get them under control. Fear is an extremely strong emotion and we can easily get locked into it with scary thoughts such as, "I'm sure this is worse than usual! This really is a heart attack!" So we need to know how to switch off a panic attack once we are in full flow.

The sensations associated with a panic attack are the same, whether they are induced by a particular overload of stress, a fear of particular places, a fear of being outside the home (agoraphobia) or of behaving unacceptably in public places or certain settings (social phobias). Therefore, the method below can be applied, whatever the circumstance.

First, you need to stop the excess carbon dioxide loss

If you recall, when you breathe in short breaths or gasps but don't take any physical action, you take in more oxygen than you can use and it gets breathed out again, taking carbon dioxide with it. But oxygen can't be absorbed by body tissues without the help of carbon dioxide, so if too much carbon dioxide is lost in this way, you suffer the terrifying feeling of choking or suffocating, even though you are still taking in air. You can stop excess carbon dioxide loss in one of these ways:

- *Hold your breath and count to 10*
- *Start 7/11 breathing* (see page 103)
  When your out-breath is longer than your in-breath, you are stopping yourself from gasping and are thus delaying the next intake of oxygen that you couldn't use. As soon as you start to breathe in slowly through your nose, you'll find you lose that sensation of suffocation. If you run out of puff before you reach the count of 11, just hold your breath and continue the count, then breathe in again for 7.

Some health professionals still recommend breathing in and out of a paper bag, held over the nose and mouth. The effect is that this makes you breathe in again the precious excess carbon dioxide you have just breathed out. However the danger is that, if you carry this on for too long, you will get too little oxygen and too much carbon dioxide, leading to carbon dioxide poisoning. (This can lead to dizziness, nausea, headaches, vomiting and rapid breathing. In severe cases this might progress to confusion, convulsions and loss of consciousness.) You might also feel rather a fool breathing in and out of a paper bag in a public place. The 7/11 (or 3/5) breathing is unobtrusive and completely safe. However, if you find it easier to turn off the panic when you have something to concentrate on holding, by all means use the paper bag. But stop as soon as you feel able to switch to 7/11 breathing.

- *Do something active*

  If you find calming down difficult in such situations, another option is to take vigorous exercise instead! It may seem a ludicrous idea, if you feel you can't breathe – for how on earth could you take exercise of any kind, let alone the vigorous variety? – but just try it and see how, almost miraculously, the panicky feelings subside. This is because you are using your quick breathing for the purpose it was originally intended – to help you take swift action.

  So run up and down the stairs a few times, jog on the spot, dance to the radio, run round the block. You'll not only feel better; you'll have proof that you are not having a heart attack!

  > 66 ... it's almost miraculous how the panicky feelings subside. 99

Joe once helped a woman who was terrified that the constricting pain she experienced in her chest when she became anxious was caused by angina. Her mother had suffered from angina and she herself had now reached the age that her mother had been when the angina began. She had been checked out several times by her doctor and at the hospital and was assured there were no signs of angina. But that didn't stop her worrying. Every time she got anxious, she experienced the same pain and was convinced that, *this* time, the angina was starting. Because she had had her latest check at the doctor's surgery only the day before, Joe felt confident enough to induce a panic attack in the woman and then went running with her up the hill near his house. She was both amazed and relieved to find that the pain disappeared instantly and completely.

Encourage yourself

It is really important when an attack starts to swap negative thoughts for positive ones. Instead of driving up your panic with thoughts of dying, fainting or having an embarrassing accident, try some of the following:

- "I *can* get through this."
- "I don't like this but I know it is going to pass if I calm down."
- "I know nothing terrible is going to happen really, I've been here before."
- "I can stop this in its tracks."
- "I am going to concentrate on counting my in-breath and out-breath."
- "I can turn this off like a tap."

Better still, come up with some good ones of your own.

Distance yourself from the panic

Try to become aware, as an observer, of what is going on in your body and then name it: "I am panicking". This can be an extremely powerful means of getting the sensations under control. Late one night, as a result of an undiagnosed illness, the husband of one of our colleagues started coughing up blood through his mouth and nose (the latter itself a result of panic, although they didn't realise it at the time). It was, understandably, an extremely frightening experience for them both. She called an ambulance and tried to calm her husband, then found herself shaking and struggling to breathe. She remembers saying to herself, "I'm panicking. This isn't going to help me help Tom." Observing herself in that way was sufficient to enable her to re-focus on reassuring her husband till the ambulance arrived to take him to safe recovery in hospital.

Another helpful way to distance yourself is to put the situation into context. When Joe was a young man, he once started to have a panic attack on an underground train in London. He was taking his university finals at the time and was on his way to sit what he feared might be an especially difficult paper. He was also under stress because the rent on his digs had just gone up and a family member was unwell. As he sat on the train with panic rising, he decided to imagine extra-terrestrial life looking down on earth from the Milky Way. England would be a tiny blob, London a minute speck – and his exam room completely undetectable. Thinking this way made him laugh and put his situation into perspective.

In emergencies a tendency to put distance between oneself and the moment often arises quite naturally. Being 'in shock' is not necessarily a terrible thing. Indeed, it can be quite protective and better than getting hysterical. At the age of 15, for example, Ivan attempted to vault a horse in the gym at his school. It was high and he caught his foot on it as he went over and fell, badly breaking his left arm. Although in shock he felt calm and detached. With his left arm now stuck out at an unnatural angle and bone poking through the skin, he raised his right arm and said calmly, "Please sir! I've broken my arm." As he was led out of the hall by the grim-faced gym teacher, he still felt strangely calm and had the dreamlike experience of being amused at seeing the faces of his classmates turning white and a couple of them even fainting at the unexpected sight.

Distract yourself

Some people find it easier to concentrate hard on something such as counting leaves or bricks or paving stones (if walking in the street), or tins or cereal boxes (if in a supermarket), or reciting a favourite poem or recalling any kind of familiar list. Ideal, of course, is to get moving. If in a supermarket, you could start walking briskly up and down the aisles as if you are searching for something you have forgotten. In the street, you could just start walking fast, glancing at your watch now and then, as if in a hurry. If you are at a party, you could offer to get someone another drink or go to get one for yourself (preferably not alcohol, or not too much) or help with clearing plates and glasses for a while.

Stay in the situation

This will provide you with the best possible evidence that the circumstance you are in is not actually life-threatening at all. If you run, you are confirming for the amygdala that there was danger to flee from, and that, in such circumstances or similar ones, you had better run for it again. Whereas, if you stay and calm down, you start breaking the pattern match for next time, and you gain access to the rational part of your brain. Then you can go on to:

Consider what caused you to panic

You might want to do this straight away or later. Are you under a mounting level of stress? Did something just happen that acted as 'the last straw'? Have you had a panic attack in this place before and you've pattern matched to the previous event? Did you unwittingly induce a panic attack by thinking, "I wonder if I'm going to have a panic attack here"/"It would be terrible if I were to have a panic attack here?" When we have an explanation, the event becomes less overwhelming and frightening.

Escape if you absolutely have to

If you just cannot get a grip on controlling your panic on a particular occasion, time take out. Leave the shop. Step out of the party or the pub. Get out of the lift. Pull over in the car. But then work hard to calm yourself and, once you have thought about what might have induced the panic, go back, in your calm state, and try to carry on with what you were doing before. You will be lessening the association with danger, if you are successful this second time round. But if you just cannot carry on, don't beat yourself up with guilt about it. Treat this as a reminder to practise your self-calming techniques more.

How to reduce the risk of panic attacks

Ideally, of course, we don't want to have to cope with panic attacks but to reduce the risk of their happening altogether. The best way to overcome them is to start with the rewind technique, so as to neutralise the high emotion attached to the panic situations you have experienced in the past, and thus stop inappropriate pattern matching in the future. How therapists do this will be described in the next section. Then you will need to take the following steps, to help you recover a normal life. If rewind treatment is not available to you, you can still learn to overcome your fear of panic attacks by taking the following steps.

- *Practise 7/11 breathing every day*
- *Draw up a list of 10 feared situations*
  where 1 is one that induces mild panic (perhaps posting a letter in the box at the end of the street or meeting a friend for a coffee) and 10 is one that almost induces a panic attack at the very thought of it (shopping in a major supermarket on a crowded Saturday morning, for instance, or going to a wedding). Decide what would be a 5 Perhaps a drink with your partner in the pub on a quiet Thursday evening or eating in the canteen. Then fill in 2, 3 and 4 and 6, 7, 8 and 9 accordingly.

- *Imagine success*
  Relax yourself as deeply as you can, perhaps going in your mind to your 'special place' for a while. Then, in your imagination, see yourself calmly leaving the house and walking down to the post box with your letter (or having the coffee with your friend without spilling it or choking). Do this on a few occasions. Then go to the post box/café for real. (If your situation doesn't naturally involve another person, you can take someone with you the first time and then go another time on your own.) All the time, concentrate on remaining calm in the ways we have shown you. When you feel comfortable about doing the first activity, move on to number 2 on your list. Imagine yourself doing what needs to be done to accomplish it successfully. Then do it for real. And so you progress up your hierarchy of

fears at a steady pace, with each last success bolstering you for the next one.

Don't just imagine perfectly straightforward situations. Imagine the worst that might happen (something possible, not far-fetched and over-dramatic) and then see yourself

How to use imagination to control blushing

RELAX YOURSELF, imagine a situation in which you tend to blush and let the blush happen. Then imagine a thin, flexible film of cooling ice, pleasantly covering the skin of your face and neck. Really concentrate on the sensation of cold ice. Just as we can bring saliva into our mouths by imagining the tart taste of a lemon, so we can direct blood away from the face and neck if we create for ourselves the sensation of cold. Try this in your imagination until you can achieve the effect reliably without closing your eyes. (Check it out in the mirror.) Then apply it whenever you are in a situation in which you feel a blush rising.

Another approach is to imagine a situation that makes you blush with embarrassment or anxiety and then 'instruct' your brain to signal for even more blood to come rushing to your face and neck. Get yourself blushing redder than you have ever blushed before. (If you dare do it in public once or twice, even better.) What happens if you do this is that, when the thinking part of your brain instructs the brainstem to make you as red as a pillar box (when usually, at the first flush, you would turn and flee), it cottons on to the fact that the situation can't be so dangerous after all. So gradually it turns off the blushing response altogether.

coping successfully with the crisis. For instance, perhaps you might imagine someone jogging your arm in the pub, making you spill your drink on a stranger's coat. You see yourself apologising profusely but calmly, offering to pay for dry-cleaning, if necessary, and so on. If the imagined person refuses to be mollified, hear yourself saying firmly, "I am truly sorry for spoiling your evening and I am happy to give you the money for dry-cleaning" and then moving away. And see yourself calmly repeating this, if the person keeps making a point of complaining.

- *Expect setbacks*

It is unlikely that you will progress right through your list without a glitch. But don't think you have to go right back to number 1, if you balk at no 6. Think instead about *why* you might have had difficulty (perhaps you had just had some bad news; perhaps you hadn't slept well the previous night), so you were already more stressed than usual when you went into a situation that, by its very inclusion on your list, could be expected to be somewhat stressful. Use the knowledge that the circumstances were unusual or else explicable in some way to help you try again.

- *Take control*

Feeling helpless and at the mercy of a feared situation is part of what makes panic escalate. Remember, it is a human need to feel in control, so have some coping tactics ready for particular situations. If you are going to the theatre or cinema or somewhere similar, ensure you know where the exits are and how to reach them. If you are going to give a presentation, have a few questions in mind that you could ask your audience, momentarily to take the attention away from you if your anxiety starts to rise. Or tell the audience that you feel a little nervous – nothing is better guaranteed to get them on your side! We like other people to admit being 'human', just like us. And if you take control of your situation in such ways, by creating the means of temporary escape, you are less likely to need them.

For sufferers from social phobia, the cause of blushing or shaking or clamming up is often an over-focus on oneself. In effect, the person is thinking, "What is he/she going to think about *me/my* behaviour/*my* performance? Will they think I am stupid, overdressed, under-dressed, etc.?" It is most salutary to realise that they probably aren't thinking about you in those ways at all. They might well be more interested in the impact *they* are making! So, a highly effective way to take some control and feel more relaxed is to ask questions of other people. Get them talking about themselves, what they do, what they like, what they think about certain things. All people like

> **" It is most salutary to realise that other people probably aren't thinking about you at all. "**

to be asked about themselves or their opinions, and will probably think warmly of you for doing so.*

- *Remind yourself*

Write out on a card a reminder of what you need to do. This is a cognitive technique known by the acronym AWARE.[†]

Accept – don't fight the panic because you will make it worse. Breathe calmly;

Watch – try to stand outside what is happening and observe it. Scale it for severity from 1 to 10;

Act – normally. Try not to do anything to escape, as that will bring only short-term relief;

Repeat – go back over the first three steps and check that you are still doing them, instead of tensing up and getting more frightened

Expect – the best. Don't catastrophise, as that exacerbates symptoms. Be confident that this will pass in moments, if you allow it to.

---

* Often people are fearful of social occasions because they haven't, for one reason or another, learned good social skills. The good news is that these can be learned at any age. One sympathetic and simple self-help book is *Be the Life and Soul of the Party: socialising for success* by Clare Walker, Crown House Publishing, 2005.

† Beck, A., Emery, G. and Greensberg, R. (1985) *Anxiety Disorders and Phobias*. Basic Books.

- *Put aside fear of embarrassment*

For many people, the single reason most likely to cause their
panic to escalate is the fear that their behaviour will be uncontrollable and so out of place and unacceptable that other people will think they are crazy. If we realised just how common
panic attacks are, we would stop being so embarrassed about
what other people might think of them! A large number of the
people you come across will have had one at some time too.

> *Remember: a panic attack is not a sign of mental illness.
> It is a statement about the stress levels in your life.*

Eleanor rides out a relapse

Eleanor was a 50-year-old woman who had suffered from
agoraphobia for some years. With Joe's help, she had advanced very successfully up her hierarchy of fears and had actually reached '9' – which, for her, was visiting the supermarket
on a moderately busy day. But the day after achieving that,
she rang Joe in a total panic. She couldn't now even go outside the door, she said. What had happened in the interim
was that she had found out that her husband's firm was to
be relocated from just around the corner to a town 30 miles
away. It had always helped her to know that she could call on
him if she suffered a terrible panic and he would be able to get
to her to help her. First, she begged him to leave the firm.

Then, she begged him to stay with it, because they had four children to support. Then again she begged him to give up the job, and then once more she changed her mind. She was in a terrible state.

Joe asked her to have someone drive her to his office, where he calmed her down. He then told her that it was absolutely normal to want there to be someone she could call on if she was frightened. Was there anyone else she could rely on, instead of her husband? As Eleanor could now think straight, she was able to realise that her husband wasn't the only possible source of support. One of her neighbours knew about her panic attacks and had always been very sympathetic. She could call on her. And her sister lived quite close too. It probably wouldn't be an onerous responsibility for either of them because, as she could now acknowledge, she never actually had to call on her husband at all. What was important for her was knowing that he was there.

"Joe, do I have to go all the way back down to 1 and start over again, now? Have I ruined all I achieved so far?" she said.

"The very fact that you ask the question in that way tells you the answer is no," he told her. "Once you have learned a skill, you have it available to you if you choose to use it – just like riding a bike."

> " Once you have learned a skill you always have it available to you ... "

Matthew changes perspective

Matthew was 18 when he came to see Joe because of a terror of eating in public. He was going away to university, where he would stay in a hall of residence that offered subsidised meals in its canteen. He didn't know how he could possibly cope. In fact, he was so distraught that he felt life wasn't worth living anymore. "It is pointless going on. My whole life is ruined," he said. He rated his distress at a 10, top of the scale. Matthew found it difficult to imagine himself, while relaxed, having a different emotional response. So Joe tried another tack. He asked him about his interests.

"Well," he said, when Matthew had told him how he enjoyed spending his time, "you say your life is ruined. Yet you still enjoy playing football. And driving. And music. And you enjoy your studies."

"Yes, I do."

"How much time do you spend eating, in a day?"

Matthew shrugged. "About an hour."

"About an hour? So that is one twenty-fourth of a day? Because you feel uncomfortable for one twenty-fourth of a day, you think your life is ruined and you are prepared to kill yourself?"

"Well, that feels different, looking at it that way," marvelled Matthew. "I thought my whole life was ruined but it is only one twenty-fourth of it."

"So," said Joe. "You scaled your anxiety at a 10 when you arrived. What is it now?"

"It's a 2," said Matthew. "And a 2 is something I can handle." He completed his university education without further problem.

Obsessive-compulsive behaviour

Obsessive-compulsive disorders (OCD), like other anxiety disorders, are triggered off when stress rises too high to cope with, leaving significant needs unmet. But even if a need becomes met (you get over a relationship break-up and meet someone new; you find a new job or get promotion), the habit may remain because, just like any other addictive activity, it is hard to break without conscious effort. It is as if the behaviour has a life of its own and you still have to deconstruct it bit by bit. So you must actively target it, as well as working to get your lifestyle balance right. Here's how.

Treat OCD as a bully

Because that is what it is. Bullies say, "Do this or I'll hurt you". So you do whatever it is. But then they threaten again, another time, and again. They never let you go free. Well, OCD is bullying you into washing your hands 100 times a day or reciting psalms in a set order or counting how many cars go past before you get to the end of the street, as the price for preventing a feared event. And then it does it again. And again. It *doesn't* keep you safe or stop the worry of terrible things happening. All it does is blackmail you, raising the stakes, extending the punishment and still not letting you go free.

So recognise that OCD is nothing more than a parasitical bully and resolve to take back control.

Separate yourself from the OCD thought

This is powerful. When the fearful thought flashes into your mind ("My children might die if I don't go back home and check that the smoke alarm is still functioning"; "I'll get a terrible disease if I don't wash my hands after touching the newspaper/coins/doorknob"), recognise it as an OCD thought. Actually say to yourself, "That is an OCD thought. It is *not* a genuine thought" and push it out of your mind. If you stand back from it in this way and don't engage with it, it loses its power. Then, if you don't give it any further attention, the associated anxiety will stay mild and quickly disappear.

Refocus your attention

Immediately focus your attention on something else, so that the OCD can't get house room in your brain. Have activities or responses prepared in advance that you can do immediately the thought comes into mind. It should be something pleasurable or satisfying. Perhaps put on some music and do exercises to it or dance to it in your front room or bedroom. Sing a song out loud that you know a lot of the words to. Call a friend. At work, phone a colleague or make a round of tea. Do 7/11 breathing, subvocalising the numbers as you go; jump up and down on the spot; run up and downstairs. But be careful that you vary the activity. You do not want to create a new compulsive ritual.

Call its bluff

As you stop doing the rituals, you will discover that nothing bad actually happens. (You knew it wouldn't, of course, but it's only when you are not in the grip of the OCD thought that you can see that. If you let it take you over, however, you won't have access to your thinking brain at all, which is why someone can possibly entertain the ludicrous idea that, for instance, touching their left ear and then their right 50 times without a break will stop a plane from crashing.) The important thing is that, when you are emotionally aroused and you *still* don't do the ritual, the amygdala will then also realise that the ritual is *not* what alleviates the anxiety. The more you avoid performing the ritual – not by getting tense and resisting but by dismissing the thought and concentrating on something else instead – the more

> **"** ... your amygdala will then also realise that the ritual is not what alleviates the anxiety. **"**

the connection between the thought and the ritual will fade. And, as nothing life-threatening is happening as a result, the amygdala soon stops getting alarmed by the thought, and the thought fades too.

Make sure that you can calm yourself very quickly with 7/11 breathing and then try it out. And, trust yourself. Trust that you can beat this bully.

Avoid seeking reassurance

Because not performing an obsessive ritual can be so highly anxiety-arousing, people sometimes desperately try other means of getting for themselves the same, albeit illusory, 'peace of mind'. So, try not to resort to ploys such as saying to someone else, "It won't really matter if I have left the back door unlocked, will it?" "I won't really get ill if I don't wash my hands after touching that newspaper, will I?" "The window is locked, isn't it?" "No car crash was reported on the radio this afternoon, was it?" Your intention must be not to assuage the irrational anxiety but to experience it at a low level, cope with it by preventing it from escalating, and realise you can let it go.

Lee and the spare parts

Lee's OCD started when he reached 40. His father had died of a heart attack at the age of 40 and Lee was secretly terrified that this would happen to him too. He worried about how his wife and young family would cope and the financial problems he also had. So the day came when he had his first panic attack and assumed it was a heart attack. His doctor reassured him that his heart was fine and that he was fit and healthy. But his amygdala was by now hyper-aroused and he started to look for different reasons to explain the constant background of fear. Lee worked in a garage, where he was in charge of the spare parts division, and the OCD almost cost him his job. When customers were leaving the garage after work had been done on their cars, the thought would suddenly occur to him that he might have supplied the wrong part to be fitted. He would imagine their car skidding on a road or catching fire and burning its occupants to death. The anxiety induced was so extreme that he would feel impelled to run after customers and ask them to return, while he checked the new part against the stock, to ensure it was the right one. This regular occurrence became extremely annoying, both to customers and the garage owners.

Then, while driving home from work, the thought would occur to him that he might have knocked someone down without realising it. The thought of someone lying, bleeding or unconscious on the lonely country road, was so horrific that he felt compelled to drive slowly back almost all the 30 miles to the garage, to ensure that no one was lying injured on the road. Not surprisingly, this was causing him to arrive home late every night.

> **Remember, OCD is a reaction to stress and unmet needs ...**

In their first therapy session, Joe taught Lee how to relax and gave him a tape of the session, with the instruction that he must drive straight home without deviation and listen to the tape at once. While Lee was still relaxed in the therapy room, Joe encouraged him to imagine himself successfully doing this, instead of turning back to retrace his route. Because the instruction tapped into Lee's tendency towards obsessive behaviour, he was able to do this and, after a couple of weeks, during which time there were no stories in the local newspaper of fatalities caused by hit-and-run drivers, that particular obsessive thought faded away.

Dealing with the spare parts ritual was more complex as Lee became so emotionally aroused when the thought of supplying the wrong part occurred to him that he couldn't bear not to check his work. Joe therefore suggested that they should break the problem down into chunks and deal with each one in turn. The first step was not to try to stop the ritual but to dilute it. Lee agreed to keep a notepad with him and note down the number of each spare part when he handed it out. Then, instead of running after customers and alarming and annoying them, when the anxiety came upon him, he would go to the stock room and check the number in his notepad against the stock. This wasn't as satisfying but it settled his anxiety and, after a few weeks of this, that obsessive thought and the need for the ritual had disappeared too.

Lee had other more minor rituals too and, all in all, it took 12 sessions of therapy to deal with the whole constellation. During that time, Joe used the rewind technique, helped him to visualise success and helped him to find ways to focus outwards and distract himself from irrational, fearful thoughts. However, Lee's last obsessive activity was listening to Joe's relaxation tape! So, to help him with this, Joe suggested he start listening to it on alternate nights, then once a week and then only when he felt anxious and gradually the need for it stopped.

OCD, in any other form

Remember, OCD is a reaction to stress and unmet needs and it can come back in another form at another time, if these rise to a higher level than you can cope with.

For instance, Ivan once worked with a conscientious young builder called Chris, who had developed the need to check repeatedly that he had properly locked up the windows and doors of the properties where he was working. This tendency was always particularly bad when he was stressed because of the uncertainties of his business. And as he tended to work on several jobs at once, he often spent hours every day and evening in a trance, locking and unlocking and locking again, "just to make sure".

Ivan quickly helped Chris to cope with the symptoms by teaching him the skills we've described above and getting him to address his stressful circumstances in a practical way. The OCD faded away. Some years later, Chris called Ivan again. The OCD was back. He had developed another compulsion but this time based around asbestos. He couldn't get over the thought that, whenever he was demolishing parts of buildings, there might be asbestos present. He had been affected by the many health scare stories concerning asbestos but had not registered that most forms of asbestos are quite harmless. So now he was changing clothes and showering several times a day after the merest hint that he might possibly have been anywhere near asbestos.

During therapy it emerged that everything had been going well till a few months ago, when his wife had had their first baby and, at the same time, a firm for which he was working as a sub-contractor went bankrupt, owing him over £21,000. The sleepless nights and responsibilities of being a new dad, plus the financial stress of his business (which made him feel he should put in very long hours to make up the deficit at just the time when he also felt he should be at home supporting his new wife and baby) took their toll. His stress levels were at maximum.

Once again, Ivan was able to help Chris take control of his symptoms and insisted he take a break from work, so that he could stand back, take a bigger perspective on his situation and decide how he could best manage to reduce his stress. At first Chris resisted this strongly, saying he certainly couldn't afford to take a break and that he needed to take as many jobs as possible at knock-down prices "just to get myself out of a hole" (but in fact digging himself further into it). But, in the end, he agreed. He took a well-earned holiday. In this essential 'time out' period, he realised that working in this way only perpetuated his problems, as he never got ahead. He decided that he wasn't suited to the life of a self-employed builder and joined a local firm as a foreman. He also learned to recognise if OCD was starting to creep up on him again in some new disguised form and to take stock of his circumstances at once. (He now gives talks to OCD sufferers to show them that it is possible to overcome the condition.)

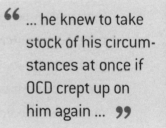

... he knew to take stock of his circumstances at once if OCD crept up on him again ...

Anxieties related to sex

There can be many reasons for feeling anxious about sex and not being able to 'perform' well or to receive pleasure. Although most causes are psychological, some may have their origin in a physical condition that has an effect on sexual performance or enjoyment. For instance, acute illnesses, chronic illnesses such as diabetes, heart disease or respiratory diseases, and conditions such as backache may impair our ability to enjoy sex – either because they make it painful or difficult or because they induce fearfulness. (Often, for instance, people with a heart condition are frightened of having a heart attack during sex.) For women, dryness of the vagina caused by sexual infection, hormonal abnormalities or allergic reaction to the rubber in a condom or cap may cause pain that makes sex an unwelcome proposition. However, this may be misinterpreted by either partner as lack of sexual interest or an inability to relax and enjoy the occasion. Taking certain prescription drugs (most notably, certain antidepressants and medication to lower blood pressure) can, as an unwanted side effect, result in loss of libido as well as, for males, inability to have or maintain an erection – the most common sexual difficulty suffered by men.

A man can quite easily find out whether failure to get an erection has physical or psychological causes. It is natural to

get erections during sleep, and most men wake from sleep
at some time with an erection. If this still occurs, the cause of
any difficulty is psychological – and temporary. Women may
think they have a physical problem if the entrance to the vagina appears to be clamped shut. In fact, although a physical
effect, it has a psychological cause (vaginismus, see below).
Sometimes sexual problems may be related to an abnormali-
ty in the functioning of the reproductive organs themselves,
which needs to be treated.

Psychological causes

Psychological explanations for sexual difficulties are the most
common. These can range from inexperience and misinfor-
mation to fear of failure and emotional problems within a
relationship.

It is natural to feel anxious if we are inexperienced at sex or
have been out of a loving relationship for a long time before
starting a new one. Unfortunately, our very anxiety to please
and/or our fear of not being able to do so creates the very circumstance that we fear – inability to focus fully either on our
partner or our own pleasure. Worry, as we know, makes it
impossible to stay in the moment and therefore to relax into
sexual enjoyment.

Often, however, it is unpleasant or traumatic past experiences of sex that cause the current difficulty. Someone who

has been sexually assaulted or raped or who has generally been treated without respect within a sexual relationship may feel reluctant – or unable – to put themselves in such a vulnerable position again. Unresolved feelings or guilt about an abortion can sometimes affect women's ability to enjoy sex. And fear of intimacy can cause anxiety in both men and women.

Vaginismus, an involuntary spasm of the muscles around the entrance to the vagina (and sometimes the thigh, stomach, anus and buttock muscles), which in effect closes it off, may occur as a result of fear of sex or a past frightening experience of sex. It most commonly affects young women under the age of 24.

Sometimes, deeper problems within a relationship may manifest themselves as loss of interest in sex (and, therefore, sometimes pain during sex). Communication failures and differences over money matters and childcare, for instance, can very often be causes of sexual difficulties, as, of course, can 'growing apart' and ceasing to share interests or values. Often, however, the sexual difficulties within an established relationship may stem from a difference in level of desire. Once the passionate, early stage of a relationship has passed, couples may well discover that one partner has a greater need or desire for sex than the other. Or one (usually the male) may use sex as a way to discharge pent-up stress, whereas the other becomes totally uninterested in sex in such circumstances.

What to do

Get information: If you are not clear about the mechanics of sex or the permutations of lovemaking, there are many good books available that can help you. Once you know what is happening in your body and what you can do to bring pleasure to yourself and a partner, you will be better able to relax and your confidence will increase.

Get help: If you think your problem may be physical, however, seek advice from your doctor. Vaginismus can be helped by reassurance that there is nothing physically wrong, by correct information about sex and by a gradual programme of introducing into the vagina, while deeply relaxed, objects other than a penis, such as a mini-tampon, finger and a thin vibrator, until confidence is built up.

Rehearse success: The key to overcoming sexual anxieties is to rehearse success. Get yourself comfortable and relaxed and then use your imagination to see yourself going through the process of making love with your partner, enjoying being with him or her, keeping your mind on their pleasure and comfort, and enjoying their responses. If you have been comfortable about sex with a previous partner or at a previous time in the relationship, take yourself back, in your imagination, to how you were at that time. Then bring that quality of confidence back into yourself now. It is a resource that remains available to you.

Talk clean: In any meaningful relationship, you have been chosen for who you are, not for your sexual performance. Your partner wants to be with you and they do not set out to judge you. A highly effective way of dispelling concerns is to share them. Tell your partner if you feel tense and nervous – after all it is flattering to know that someone cares enough to get anxious!

Hold back: If a man's difficulty is premature ejaculation, he can help himself by mentally *removing* himself from the moment and imagining something that will bring his level of sexual arousal down temporarily. Many men have done this successfully by imagining all sorts of things, from cold showers to counting backwards from 100. Be careful, however, not to think of something that is such a downer that it puts you off having sex altogether.

Ban sex (for a while): This can be helpful particularly when a feeling of pressure to have sex leads to loss of enjoyment in it. The agreement is to spend 40 minutes with your partner in intimate activity that falls short of sex but that might entail giving each other back rubs, massage with aromatherapy oils, cuddling and kissing or whatever either of you requests.

Knowing that sex will not be expected allows both partners to fully enjoy the moment and slowly build up intimacy again. Carry this on for a week and try not to break the ban, even if you both think you want to. Then, when you do have sex again, the desire is more likely to be strong and mutual.

Have the rewind treatment: If sexual problems have arisen because of a former, traumatic experience of sex, using the rewind technique to neutralise the emotion associated with that memory is to be recommended. Then, with that put safely behind you, you can start the process of learning to trust and relax sexually again with a loving partner.

Compromise: If your level of desire differs from that of your partner, it is sensible to try to reach a compromise that goes some way towards meeting the needs of you both. For instance, it can help to accept that the level of intensity experienced during sex does not always have to be equal. Also, if one partner likes sex twice a week and the other would like it to be once a fortnight (resulting in neither being happy much of the time), perhaps a good compromise would be to agree wholeheartedly on sex once a week.

Sort out problems: If a sexual problem or lack of sexual interest is rooted in a dysfunctional relationship, it is the relationship that needs sorting out, rather than the sex. Commonly, by the time a relationship has deteriorated to this

point, communication between partners is poor. A good starting point, if you can both agree it, is to set aside half an hour
when you can both express your concerns *about something
current* and negotiate to get needs met. You should take it in
turns to speak for five minutes and, while one is speaking, the
other must listen, not interrupt or speak at all. The aim is for
each person to feel heard, so your ground rules should be: no
attacks on each other's character, no bringing up of old griev-
ances and an emphasis on problem solving or compromise. If
necessary, consider couple counselling.

If you think you need more help
with your anxiety ...

Not everyone finds it easy to apply self-help measures from
a book, without someone to give them guidance and support.
If this is the case for you, please take a look at Part 3, which
offers advice on finding effective, professional help and illustrates how human givens therapist work with anxious clients.

PART 3

Seeking professional help

*M*ANY readers may, by this point, feel confident about putting into practice the effective techniques we have described for handling anxiety, in its variety of forms. But not all of us feel comfortable doing it by ourselves. When we are in the grip of anxiety, we can sometimes get tunnel vision leaving us capable of focusing on little other than our own narrow problem writ large, so we need someone else with the skills to help us put things back into proper perspective and to offer the reframes that open us up to the possibility of seeing our circumstances in a different way.

Also, as we have mentioned already, if you are still being affected by high emotional arousal due to a past traumatic event, this needs to be resolved, so that the event can be processed as a normal memory, without the attendant, incapacitating emotion. This is best done by a therapist who is proficient in the rewind technique.

Choosing a therapist is an extremely important step. There are well over 400 schools of therapy which can make it extremely difficult to know where to start. How could there

be so many permutations and practices within one professional discipline! It does seem absurd, after all there would
never be that many ways to treat a physical illness. Such
disparity, and so little shared common ground between the
approaches to psychotherapy, mean that people in the field
are themselves confused about what really works. For instance, behavioural therapists concentrate on helping people
to change their behaviour. Cognitive therapists concentrate
on the idea that changing the way anxious people think about
things will have the effect of making them change their behaviour. In person-centred therapy (the type most commonly
on offer from counsellors in GP surgeries) the belief is that
the solution lies hidden somewhere inside the suffering individual; all the therapist has to do (the theory goes) is respect-
fully keep listening to the person talk, with a few prods in
particular directions here and there, and they'll sort it all out
for themselves. Psychodynamic therapies operate from the
belief that you have to dig up all past pains and insecurities
and major disappointments to understand and overcome
anxiety disorders. These are piecemeal approaches, and some,
albeit unwittingly, may do more harm than good.

Many of these different schools of therapy have got hold of
a part of the truth but unfortunately they stick to that one part
and hone it, to the exclusion of everything else. This tends to
unbalance the work of therapists, however well-meaning,
who work from within such limited models. Of course, it is

good to set people tasks to help them change problem behaviours or to help people become aware of and question negative thinking, or to listen to people with empathy, *but none of these approaches is sufficient on its own.*

The human givens approach to psychotherapy and counselling* is *not* piecemeal. It is an holistic approach with one strong over-arching idea at its core: we cannot be anxious or depressed or phobic or in the grip of any other form of mental ill-health if our needs are being fully met and we are making proper use of our innate resources. Human givens therapists don't diagnose deficiencies in a *person* but rather the deficiencies in their lives or circumstances that prevent them from meeting their essential needs and/or using their innate guidance system effectively to meet those needs. Having established what is required, we then use a variety of tried and tested techniques to help people achieve that end, as quickly as

> ❝ The main focus of human givens therapy is to help people get their needs met. ❞

possible. Unlike so many other schools of psychotherapy, we don't have one 'model' that we stick to like limpets and which we force everyone that comes to see us to fit. We work with what we see and learn from the individual in front of us.

---

* To find the nearest human givens therapist to you, visit: www.hgi.org.uk/register/ or call the Human Givens Institute on +44 (0)1323 811662. For information about training in the approach, visit: www.humangivenscollege.com

How to find an effective counsellor

People are often confused by the difference between the terms psychotherapist and counsellor, as they will come across both. But, essentially, there is no difference between them. How practitioners style themselves is usually just a matter of personal preference (for instance, some think the term counsellor sounds more friendly; others might think the term psychotherapist sounds more professional).

Newspaper and magazine articles on the subject of seeking therapy usually recommend that you check the register of certain organisations that accredit or register psychotherapists and counsellors. But, although well intentioned, this is not necessarily the best advice. How much training people have had, or which professional bodies they belong to, gives you no guarantee of their effectiveness as a therapist. Indeed, if practitioners stick rigidly to one model of therapy, as described above, they are not at all likely to be as effective as they could be.

The main point to remember is that whether people call themselves psychotherapists or counsellors, they will all encounter the same range of human distress in their work. All that really matters is how effective they are at helping other people.

Effective counselling checklist

We stress that an effective psychotherapist or counsellor will:

- understand depression and how to lift people out of it

- help immediately with anxiety problems including trauma (post-traumatic stress disorder) or other fear-related symptoms

- be prepared to give advice if needed or asked for

- not use jargon or 'psychobabble'

- not dwell unduly on the past

- be supportive when difficult feelings emerge, but not encourage people to remain in an emotionally aroused state

- assist individuals in developing social skills (when appropriate), so that their needs for affection, friendship, pleasure, intimacy, connection to the wider community, etc. can be better fulfilled

- help people to draw on their own resources (which may prove greater than they thought)

- be considerate of the effects of counselling on the people close to the individual concerned

- induce and teach deep relaxation

- help people think about their problems in a new and more empowering way

- use a wide range of techniques

- may set tasks to be done between sessions

- take as few sessions as possible

- increase self-confidence and independence and make sure clients feel better after every consultation.

Therapists who work with the human givens (whether or not they are human givens therapists) always work in these ways. There are some other important aspects to consider too, when making your choice.

Spare capacity

Whatever type of therapist you see, you need to be sure that they have the 'spare capacity' to work with you. Someone who is preoccupied with their own personal concerns or troubles will not be able to distance themselves sufficiently to work with yours. You will have to use your own judgement and instinct in deciding whether this is the case or not, but there is much to be gleaned from someone's manner – are they relaxed, warm and comfortable to be with, for instance, or slightly anxious or brittle? Do they give you their full attention or are they too full of themselves and seeking attention from you? Or are they perhaps too keen to push you to talk about (or not talk about) certain issues, which may reflect their own unresolved concerns? Remember, the therapist's responsibility is to work to help you. You should not feel that you need to accommodate the therapist.

Your reality, not theirs

Some people think that they need to see a therapist who comes from the same background or has the same sort of life experience, or has even experienced the same kind of trauma or discrimination as they themselves have – otherwise how will the therapist understand where they are 'coming from'? But this is quite irrelevant in the human givens approach. Because the emphasis is on what clients can do to meet their *own* needs, human givens therapists can work with anyone. What you wish to achieve or change in your life is *your* decision. It doesn't make any difference whether you are younger or older, from a

> 66 ... the therapist's responsibility is to work to help you. 99

different ethnic background, have a different religion or a different sexual orientation from the therapist you see. You establish, with their help, which needs are not being met in *your* life and set *your* own goals. The reality or world they are concerned with is yours, not theirs.

Working the way the brain works

High on the list of our important 'givens' is the ability to relax and imagine and think creatively. Human givens therapists 'tap into' their clients' innate ability to relax deeply and make use of that relaxed state to introduce positive suggestions and ideas, as well as helping them use their imaginations to rehearse success in new skills. When you are relaxed, the right (visual, more intuitive) hemisphere of your brain is dominant, while the left hemisphere (which is more involved in language, analysis and rational thought) takes a break. It is the right hemisphere that is active when we dream, and its natural way of working is through metaphor. (We are using metaphor whenever we say something tastes, looks or sounds *like* something else.) Metaphors conjure up pictures and sensations that the more imaginative right hemisphere can instantly relate to. And by bypassing the often resistant or negative rational part of our brains, we can take on board new ideas and useful analogies.

This is why metaphor is used a great deal in the human givens approach. To a young woman who loves nature and who has struggled throughout her life because of childhood abuse, talk of 'rooting' new ideas or 'fertile soil in which a fragile flower can at last flourish and grow strong' can be powerful indeed. Similarly, someone who is held back in their work life through their fear of taking risks, and who happens to be a keen swimmer, may respond to the idea of 'taking the plunge' and an image of rivers flowing freely. Stories are the kings and queens of metaphor, and much can be achieved instantly, with an apposite tale, that might otherwise have taken weeks. Tales of overcoming misfortune, heroic acts, kindness that triumphs, loyalty that never wavers, dreams that, with hard work and belief, come true – these connect with us through our natural pattern-matching facility and lead us unconsciously to make the link between the metaphor or story and our life.

The rewind technique – a speedy treatment for psychological trauma and phobias

All human givens therapists are taught how to use the rewind technique*, a safe and swift method of neutralising high emotional arousal which has prevented the memory of a traumatic event from being processed as something that is in the past. Thus the trauma continues to impinge on everyday life in the form of intrusive memories, nightmares and constant unidentified anxiety (see the explanation of post-traumatic stress disorder, PTSD, on page 47 in Part 1).

We, and other human givens therapists, have used the technique with great success, and often in one session, to resolve PTSD caused by traumas such as being caught up in rail disasters, bomb attacks, near drownings, burning houses, horrific industrial accidents, vicious personal attacks, severe

---

* The original version of this technique was developed by the founders of NLP in America after studying the hypnotic techniques of Milton H. Erickson. By discovering *why* it worked we were able to adapt and refine the technique to ensure more consistent results.

sexual and physical abuse and so on. It is also a successful means of eliminating the high anxiety associated with phobias, obsessively carrying out compulsive rituals and fear of panic attacks. The rewind technique should only be carried out by an experienced practitioner. (See box below.)

The stages of the rewind technique

THE REWIND technique is performed when you are in a state of deep relaxation. Once you are calm and deeply relaxed, you are asked to recall or imagine a place where you feel totally safe and, with the aid of the therapist's promptings, to 'see' (for instance, the white sandy beach, the pale blue sea, the snow-covered mountains), 'hear' (for instance, the breaking of waves, the rustle of leaves, birds singing) 'smell' (for instance, the salty air, the perfume of flowers) and 'experience the textures' (for instance, the feel of the sand between your toes, the touch of a leaf) that you associate with that place.

You are asked to imagine that a TV set and a video or DVD player with a remote control facility appears in the beautiful surroundings you have conjured up in your imagination. Next you are asked to 'float' to one side of yourself, out of your body, and to watch yourself watching the screen, without actually seeing the picture. (This the therapist calls 'a double dissociation' and is a means of creating significant emotional distance from the traumatic memories so they can be approached relatively calmly.)

You are then asked to watch yourself watching a 'film' ▶

of the traumatic event, or of one of the occasions when your phobia made you extremely frightened, speeded up in fast forward mode. The film begins at a point before the event occurred when you didn't know anything terrible was about to happen and ends at a point at which the event is over and you feel safe again.

You are then asked, in your imagination, to float back into your body and experience yourself going swiftly backwards through the traumatic memory, from safe point to safe point, as if you were a character in a video that is being rewound. Then you watch the same images but as if on the TV screen while pressing the fast forward button.

All this is repeated back and forth, as quickly as possible, and as many times as needed, till the scenes evoke no emotion in you.

If the treatment is being applied to deal with a phobia, you will rewind a number of memories of when you experienced the phobic responses really intensely.

Afterwards, if the feared circumstance (whether trauma- or phobia-based) is one that will be confronted again in the future – for instance, driving a car, using the underground or encountering a dog – you are asked, while still relaxed, to imagine a scenario in which you are feeling relaxed and confident whilst doing so.

Besides being safe, quick and painless, this technique has the advantage of being non-voyeuristic. Intimate details you do not want to talk about – or any details at all – can remain private, because they are your memories and it is only *you* who watches the 'film'.

In Part 1, we explained how and why the method works so successfully and also mentioned that there are other speedy ways of resolving trauma that work in the same way – eye movement desensitisation reprocessing (EMDR), thought field therapy (TFT) and emotional freedom therapy (EFT), known colloquially as 'tapping'.

We personally favour the rewind technique, however, because, through lengthy experience, we know that a skilled therapist can use the technique to detraumatise a whole range of traumas in just one rewind, without these needing to be verbalised in turn or even necessarily brought to consciousness – something cognitive behavioural therapy (CBT) has never been able to do. Another advantage of the rewind technique is that a profound level of calmness is induced in the patient *beforehand*, with the effect that arousal can more easily be kept down once the patient gets in touch with the traumatic event. We also monitor patients' emotional state closely and, if arousal increases, we can guide them to take a break from 'viewing' the traumatic event and return in their imagination to the 'safe place' identified prior to starting the procedure. In this way we have a means of preventing a person from becoming too fearful and emotional,

> " ... a skilled therapist can use the rewind technique to detraumatise a whole range of traumas in just one session ... "

which is absolutely crucial for the success of the technique. Also, it is easy to integrate other therapeutic procedures with the rewind technique, such as the use of empowering metaphors and storytelling, while the person is still in a deeply relaxed state and the rehearsing of new learning, as described above.

However, it is important to be aware that, although the rewind technique has a higher success rate than any other treatment we know of, we occasionally come across people for whom it doesn't work so well or doesn't work at all – particularly people who have difficulty relaxing deeply or getting in touch with feelings associated with the original trauma. People on the autistic spectrum, for example, whose brains don't seem to store, or have access to, specific emotional memories in the usual way, do not always seem to respond well to this treatment.

Therapy that works

As we have seen, the human givens approach takes into account the full range of human nature and needs. So, to give you a flavour of how therapy from this approach works, in the following pages we describe how various human givens therapists have helped people with a range of anxiety disorders.

When the flashbacks finally stopped

When 32-year-old Beth came for an assessment interview with consultant psychiatrist Dr Farouk Okhai, she was full of nervous energy, was clearly extremely distressed and anxious, and went into great detail when answering questions. She was afraid that her problems wouldn't be taken seriously, as she looked well, had a decent job and had also just got married two weeks previously to a man she adored. However, because she feared her new husband would be hurt and also that he might want to discuss her past with him in detail (which she was reluctant to do), she hadn't told him that she was coming to therapy. She was desperately hoping her marriage would be a turning point in her life, and wanted to get on top of the things that she was struggling to cope with.

Once she realised that Farouk was not going to be dismissive of her, she was able to calm down a little and tell her story. Her mother was a drug addict, who had been hospitalised at one time, and her father had been excessively strict. As a young child, she had been terrified of his tirades and his violence against her. At just five years old, she was taken to hospital with suspicious bruising on her face and placed on the 'at risk' register. Later, after being badly beaten with a belt and ending up in hospital, she was taken into foster care and then put into a children's home, where she was sexually abused. Eventually, she went to live with her grandparents. This was the happiest time in Beth's life and she was devastated, at 15, when her grandmother died.

In spite of difficulties at school, including being bullied, Beth managed to go on to college and, since then, had had a number of generally unsatisfactory clerical jobs. At 21 she became pregnant but, as her partner at the time was not supportive, after much agonising, she had decided on an abortion. After telling all this to Farouk, Beth said, "I have overwhelming feelings that I find hard to pinpoint one at a time because they are linked together by emotions that have stayed with me – rejection, self-blame, failure, insecurity, the feeling that it's *me* and I deserve whatever happens in my life." She then went on to explain how she was often overwhelmed by these emotions which were triggered by a raised or critical voice, a 'look' or a hand gesture that most people would judge to be innocent. She would flinch and feel as if she were a child about to be beaten. She also tended to flinch when her husband came close to her, a response she attributed to the sexual abuse she had experienced as a child. Although she did not experience visual flashbacks, she would often be "back in my childhood with all the emotions I had then". Farouk decided that Beth's symptoms were consistent with chronic PTSD.

Six months passed between the assessment and the first

appointment (a dismayingly long time but sadly fairly routine within the NHS). At that appointment, they agreed on three goals: to deal with automatic reactions such as flinching when her husband came close; to deal with the flashbacks related to the bullying and beatings by her father when she was a child; and to deal with the guilt she felt over the abortion.

In human givens therapy, the therapist always does something in a session to make the patient feel better and more hopeful. So, in the first session, Farouk decided to address the flashbacks of the sexual abuse. When he asked Beth to scale them from 1 to 10, with 10 being the worst they could possibly be, she gave them a 10. He then took her through the rewind technique (see page 214), asking her to visualise, in turn, as many specific incidents connected with the abuse as she felt she needed to. He also taught her the 7/11 breathing technique to slow her breathing and thus help her calm down when she was anxious.

A week later, at her next session, Beth scaled the flashbacks of the abuse at between 6 and 7. Farouk wasn't surprised that they hadn't disappeared entirely as the procedure sometimes needs to be repeated. However, she said she didn't want to use the rewind technique to go through the sexual abuse incidents again. Instead, she wanted to deal with the flashbacks related to the treatment she had suffered at the hands of her father. The following week she scaled the flashbacks of sexual abuse at 2 and said those relating to her father had eased off to 7 from the 10 they had started at.

In that third session, Farouk and Beth also talked about her guilt and distress over the abortion. Even though the guilt felt all enveloping to her, she had clearly been traumatised by the procedure itself (which often remains a vivid memory). So he decided to use the rewind technique to deal with that too. Although Beth became distressed during the procedure, and felt nauseous at times, Farouk made sure she was calm before she left.

> 66 Two weeks later her rating of the distressing memories had fallen from '10' to '3'... 99

Two weeks later, Beth informed him that the distressing memories of the abortion had fallen to 3 from her original rating of 10 on the 10-point scale. The flashbacks about her father were now at 4 and those relating to the sexual abuse still at 2. She didn't want to repeat any of the rewind procedures. So, instead, they talked about her difficulties with assertiveness at work. Farouk gave her a sheet explaining simple steps to being assertive and suggested she role play some scenarios with her husband, each taking turns at being the bully and then being Beth.

He reinforced these ideas with a guided visualisation. First he relaxed Beth and then encouraged her to see herself acting assertively in different settings. While she was still deeply relaxed, he also gave her the post-hypnotic suggestion that she could induce relaxation whenever she felt anxious just by gently squeezing together her thumb and forefinger.

Beth missed her next two sessions because of illness and a conflicting appointment but, when she came back a month later, she was pleased to tell Farouk that she had successfully put the assertiveness techniques into practice, saying a firm 'No' to a colleague at work, who was often unreasonably demanding. The following session a fortnight later turned out to be their last. Beth looked well and agreed that she was more relaxed in general. She had found squeezing her thumb and forefinger when she felt stressed enormously helpful, and had been assertive in some quite difficult situations, without feeling put upon and victimised any longer. She had stopped having flash-backs of any kind and announced happily that she didn't think she needed to see Farouk anymore. She left feeling highly confident that she was going to be able to put her whole heart into her marriage and her future: she was considering training to be a teacher. It was clear that eliminating the intrusive memories had enabled her to get on with, and be optimistic about, her life.

> " She had stopped having flashbacks of any kind. "

Breaking the worry cycle

Marianne came to see Denise when she was in the final year
of a degree course and couldn't concentrate on her work. She
worried constantly – about performing poorly, about letting
herself and her family down and about illness. Her father and
mother had both had cancer and she was anxious about their
health and her own – she feared she might get cancer too. She
knew worrying didn't help but, as she put it, "If I fuss about
it, perhaps it won't really happen. But, if it does, it won't catch
me unprepared."

Their discussion revealed, however, that she wasn't 'prepared' at all, as her worrying was completely unproductive.
Denise pointed out that one could never know what life has
in store but that risks to health can be significantly reduced if
one is 'prepared' to take certain lifestyle steps such as eating
sensibly, exercising, not smoking, getting enough sleep and
not overstressing oneself – all of which serve to bolster the
body's immune system. Marianne took the point.

She decided that her goals were to get more work done (as
measured by meeting her course assignment deadlines,
which she had been failing to do) and to start creating a
healthier, more fulfilling lifestyle for herself. She spent so
much time worrying and procrastinating and then working
long hours in a rush to get work done that she didn't eat
properly, take regular exercise – or have fun.

Marianne's current practice was to stay up till the early hours, either working on overdue essays or sending emails or surfing the internet. Or else she would be on the phone to her boyfriend, who was at a different university, discussing their arrangements to go travelling for a year, when they finished their respective courses. This often led to disagreements, which meant she then couldn't sleep and couldn't get up in the morning. When she eventually surfaced, she would sit around in her dressing gown drinking coffee and feeling groggy and putting off going to lectures or studying at home. The university was a 25-minute walk away but she was usually in such a rush that she had to travel by bus or train.

Marianne obsessively made lists of things to do, although she never stuck to them. She also hated to let people down. So Denise got Marianne to contract to carry out a list of agreed tasks. She would turn off the computer by 10.30 p.m. (This meant ensuring all necessary work was completed before that time.) If she spoke to her boyfriend after 10 p.m., there would be no discussion of travel arrangements. She would set an alarm clock for 8.30 a.m. and get up. She would then shower and dress, to get into 'work' mode. She would eat a healthy breakfast. She would leave time to walk to the university and make a point of noticing things around her as she did so – trees, buildings, people, etc. (As we have seen, worriers tend to spend little time enjoying the present.) This list would be pinned on the fridge door.

Having taught Marianne 7/11 breathing, Denise then relaxed her more deeply and guided her to find a 'special place' for herself which she could visualise strongly with all her senses, encouraging her to experience staying in the moment and focus on what was around her. Then she got Marianne to see herself successfully completing the tasks she had contracted to undertake. She also helped her to see that her experience of cancer had in fact been positive. Both of her parents had overcome their disease. They had taken control of it, doing what they were required to do in terms of treatment, using their energy positively and making positive lifestyle changes. But Denise was also careful to point out that, inevitably 'things happen' that we can't control. She told Marianne a story that vividly illustrated how we have to learn to distinguish between what we can influence and what we can't, and act accordingly.

> 66 After the visualisation, Marianne felt very pleasantly relaxed ... 99

After the visualisation, Marianne felt very pleasantly relaxed – a physical state she was far too unfamiliar with. She agreed on a 'worry half hour', which entailed pushing away the repetitive worries that came into her mind and 'saving' them until the requisite time – around 6.30 p.m. She also took on the challenge of enjoying the time when she wasn't working (instead of using it to worry) and to research some activities she might enjoy getting involved in.

At her second session two weeks later, she was feeling much more optimistic. When she stuck to her contract, she felt much more alert and lively, was able to carry out her work more productively and felt more confident about its quality. She liked the response this brought from her tutors. (When she slipped back, however, she didn't like the way she felt and the loss of control she experienced.) She had also decided to join a yoga class at the university and to take up salsa dancing, and had enjoyed her first sessions of each. On one weekend, she had also gone away to visit friends. Normally on these occasions she would have taken a work assignment with her, intending to make time to do some, but she never did and then felt guilty. This time she had dismissed the idea of bringing any with her at all and had concentrated on having a good time with her friends. "It was lovely not feeling guilty!" she said.

> 66 "It was lovely not feeling guilty!" 99

Denise then asked her to start becoming aware of and challenging her negative thoughts (as described in Part 2) and to report at the next session on what she discovered. She also asked her to visualise her anxiety as something she could influence. Marianne pictured it as a sheet of ice "because I feel so shaky and trembly when I'm anxious" and then imagined the sheet suddenly flowing over her and herself radiating the heat of confidence and melting it completely.

After this, Marianne came for one more session. She reported that she was amazed by how many unrecognised negative thoughts flowed through her head – doubting thoughts about her abilities and her likeability and so forth. She looked at them in her worry half hour and to her surprise found that most just couldn't be substantiated. She then told Denise that she felt confident she could now continue by herself with the techniques and ideas she had been given. So, in a final relaxation, Denise encouraged her to see how resourceful she could be when she organised herself, how much she could enjoy life when she let herself and how curious she would now find herself about what she could achieve, if she gave her full attention to her work.

A walk around the block

Early one morning, Mark received a call from a man called Nick, who said his wife Diane had not dared to leave the house for three months and they were now desperate for help. Did Mark do home visits? Having made sure that Diane herself was happy to see him, Mark agreed to visit her at her home. But when he was driving over on the appointed day, and was just 10 minutes away, he received a call on his mobile phone from a hysterical, sobbing Diane. "Please don't come! It's too much! I just can't do it."

Mark asked her if, as he was so nearly at their house, it

would be all right if he just called in to say hello. "No!" she screamed, in panic. So Mark then asked if he could speak to Nick and arranged to call in and have a brief chat with him instead. When he arrived, Diane was hiding upstairs. Mark was naturally very understanding and sympathetic to Nick about how difficult things must be for them both at the moment. As he had realised Diane was listening, he asked Nick whether he thought she might like to have a quick look at him, "to see I'm just an ordinary chap". After a moment or two, Diane agreed. They ended up having a brief chat, during which Mark sympathised about how awful it must be for her to feel so anxious and confined to the house, and told her a little about the human givens approach. He felt it particularly important to try to build a strong rapport with her, as she was so very anxious and the approach for help had not come directly from her.

After some minutes, Diane suddenly said, "Actually, I *would* like to see you for some help." So Mark arranged to come back the next week. When he returned, Diane was nowhere near as anxious as before, because of the positive connection they had already forged. As they chatted this time, Mark learned that, not only had Diane not left the house during the past three months, because of her fear of a repeat of the panic attacks she had been experiencing, but she didn't even want Nick to leave her alone in the house, and felt nauseous and ill if he had absolutely no other choice. (Nick ran his own business from home and so was at least able to continue working to some extent.) Nor could she eat unless Nick was present, as she was terrified of choking. And she also felt suicidal. She had seen her GP and a psychiatrist and had variously been told that she suffered from OCD, anorexia, agoraphobia and severe depression. Prescribed antidepressants made her feel worse. "I don't feel anyone has really talked to me or listened to me," she said. "These just feel like textbook diagnoses I've been given."

Diane was a teacher but, when her difficulties started, had resigned from her job because she had been finding it increasingly stressful. She was also worried about her elderly, disabled mother who had become more needy but whom she was now unable to even visit. On a scale of 1 (very low) to 10 (very high), she scaled her general anxiety and her fear of leaving the house at a strong 10 and her depression at a 6. She could not remember when the panic attacks had started or what particularly had been happening in her life at the time. Mark therefore

> **" When he arrived, Diane was hiding upstairs ... "**

decided that he would use the rewind technique to resolve her strong anxiety about going out and walking to the High Street. He relaxed Diane deeply and, when they had gone forward and backward through this scenario as many times as she felt she needed to, he encouraged her to visualise herself making the trip with confidence and pleasure.

Afterwards, when she opened her eyes, Mark said, "Do you feel like going for a walk?" "Okay," she said, and went to get her coat. In the hall, she called up the stairs, "Nick, I'm just going out." Nick's face appeared at the top of the banisters, his eyes wide open in amazement.

> **At his next visit, Diane announced substantial improvements ...**

Diane and Mark walked round the block, with Diane pointing out familiar places, such as the local chippie and the park and saying how nice it was to see them again. She talked of how she would like to go to the cinema again with Nick and to go on the bus to visit her mother. She thought she might like to change to part-time work, so that she could be available more often for her mother, but didn't feel confident about taking on new challenges just yet.

At Mark's next visit a week later, Diane told him she felt 30 per cent better. She was going out locally with Nick and had stopped feeling scared of choking when she ate – "I've even forgotten what it was like to feel that way". (Mark wasn't at all surprised that the eating problem had sorted itself. He often found that, when fears and phobias are linked together, working directly on one or two can let the others put themselves right.) Although Nick now went out on his own more often, Diane still felt scared of his leaving her – and part of that was a fear of his leaving her altogether, because of her problems. But her general anxiety, she said, had come down from a 10 to a 3. Again, Mark used the rewind technique with her, to resolve her anxiety about the bus visit to her mother's house and to help her feel confident about making the trip. He also worked to help lift her confidence generally.

At his next visit, a week later, Diane announced substantial improvements and that she and Nick were planning a much-needed holiday together. As Diane responded so well to the rewind technique and felt positive about it, Mark used it yet again to resolve her anxiety that Nick would leave her and then encouraged her to see herself as the independent person she had previously been – someone who didn't need to rely on others and who herself was needed. After that session, Diane felt positive about moving on with her life again.

Eighteen months later, Nick, contacting Mark about a completely unrelated concern of his own, was able to report that Diane was fully engaged with life again and training to be a massage therapist.

> **66** Nick was happy to report that she was fully engaged with life again. **99**

Batman and the Incredible Hulk

Jamie came with his mother to see Mike, after appointments with the child and adolescent mental health services team and with a hospital psychiatrist had had no positive effect. Several months ago, Jamie, a highly intelligent and imaginative 10-year-old, had nearly choked on some food while eating an evening meal with his family. The incident had been upsetting and frightening for everyone concerned, although no medical intervention or hospital treatment had been required. However, it seemed the incident had been so traumatic for Jamie himself that he appeared to have 'erased' it from his conscious memory entirely. He was well aware that he felt highly fearful at the prospect of eating any lumpy food

> Since that time, he had eaten no 'normal' solid food.

(including liquidised food that might inadvertently have lumps in it), but appeared to have no conscious recollection of why or how this had come about. His explanation was simply that he "woke up one day unable to eat lumps".

Since that time, he had eaten no 'normal' solid food. All food had to be liquidised, and the real (or imagined) presence of anything remotely resembling a 'lump' in his food induced severe symptoms of panic. As a result, he had lost significant weight over the 8–10 weeks since the incident, and his general health was beginning to suffer.

Like many young boys, Jamie was extremely interested in 'superhero' characters and science fiction. As by nature he was quite shy, with a tendency to be withdrawn and intro-spective, his fantasy world offered him somewhere safe to live an 'exciting' life in his imagination. So, to build rapport with Jamie, Mike focused on his superhero interest – Jamie soon became animated and excited as he talked about the different characters, their qualities and the way they lived their lives.

As Jamie was highly intelligent, explaining the nature of PTSD to him was easy using superhero metaphors. He quick-ly grasped the role of the amygdala when it was explained to him in terms of the Incredible Hulk acting as the 'early warning sentry' to the 'citadel' of his mind. To have one of the 'good guys' on guard duty, assessing the world for potential threat made perfect sense to him. Jamie also understood that soldiers or sentries must follow instructions 'to the letter', without thought, question or reason – so the idea that the Incredible Hulk was slavishly carrying out orders to "Repel all lumps!" – even when most lumps were harmless – also made perfect sense, and had him rolling his eyes upwards in mock exasperation at this "good guy who was a few sand-wiches short of a full picnic"!

He knew Batman, on the other hand, was in a different league all together: intelligent and quick-witted. Knowing that Batman was directing operations as the thinking part of his brain – or the 'Head of his neocortical conscious' as they agreed to term it – was very reassuring to Jamie: he knew that Batman wouldn't unthinkingly discriminate against *all* lumps, and this was a great relief to him, as, rationally, his own 'lump phobia' made no sense to him whatsoever.

So, after talking about this for a little while, Mike invited Jamie to imagine going on a journey through Middle Earth (*The Lord of the Rings* was another of his great passions), and, from a vantage point midway along the route, to watch images relating to his choking incident played on the natural projection screen of a giant cliff face. That he couldn't remember the incident was no problem – he was aware of how frightening the idea of choking on a future lump was for him, so they worked with that. Jamie interspersed the rewinding of the imagined fear of choking with a sub-plot: that of Batman 'tearing a strip' off the Hulk, advising him that he (Batman) was more than capable of deciding on a day-to-day basis which lumps were safe, and Hulk was only to intervene if a genuinely life-threatening lump appeared on the scene. This sub-plot ended with a suitably chastened Hulk resuming his guard duty.

Mike then guided Jamie on through his Middle Earth trip to his destination at the top of a mountain, where the 'safety lock' to his early warning system was kept. Next, he invited

Jamie to imagine himself setting the appropriate levels of safety and security on this early warning system, and then 'locking' the system himself so that the Hulk couldn't inadvertently mess up what he and Batman knew to be the right settings. Mike left him with the suggestion that he could trust his own 'Batman' to constantly review all settings and make appropriate changes where necessary. He also suggested that Jamie could use this in-built 'superhero' confidence in as many other areas of his life as he chose.

Jamie immersed himself in this mixture of fantasy worlds entirely; when, in his mind, he experienced himself walking up the mountain, his feet 'marched' in reality and, when the suggestion was made to 'lock' the system, his hand reached out in a key-turning action.

Returning him from his adventure, Mike guided Jamie to see himself enjoying his favourite meal with his family that very evening. His mother, who was present throughout the session, had agreed at the start that, if he wanted, the whole family would go out that evening for his favourite meal of roast

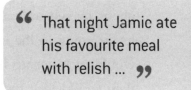

66 That night Jamie ate his favourite meal with relish ... 99

lamb and roast potatoes. While visualising this, Jamie's hands started moving as if cutting and forking food, and on several occasions he even licked his lips!

The family did go out to dinner that evening and Jamie ate

his favourite roast lamb and potatoes with relish. (Mike had told the parents that it was important that they too should have a positive expectation that the occasion would go well and not to exhibit any anxiety of their own.) Jamie has eaten 'lumpy' food ever since, with no problems whatsoever.

The carousel

A self-assured lady in her middle 50s, Joanna's life was working well except for one thing. She had always had a fear of flying, and as a consequence had never flown. Her daughter and son-in-law had emigrated to Australia and had just had a baby, and so now she would absolutely *have* to fly if she wanted to see her newborn grandson. She was completely terrified. But in this instance, there was no traumatic experience to rewind – the fears were just in her head. Desperate for help, she went to see Helen.

Looking for resources to build upon, Helen asked Joanna about herself and discovered that, as a child, Joanna had loved going to the fairground. So, she told Joanna that she would pick her up from her home the following week and they would visit the local funfair together. (If Joanna found this odd, she didn't say.) Helen led her to the carousel, with its array of painted animals that go round in a circle, bobbing up and down, and suggested they each chose one to sit astride. There they sat, two mature women on a giraffe and a horse – it was in the middle of the week, during working hours, so very few people were around, though Joanna wasn't bothered anyway. While they waited for the ride to start, Helen took the opportunity to get Joanna to slow her breathing and then, as they took off, suggested she shut her eyes and really get into the experience. Soon Joanna was completely in the moment, removing her feet from the stirrups and thrusting out her legs, and letting go of the pole with one hand.

"You know, Joanna, this is just like flying!" Helen yelled across to her. "We could be on a magic carpet now. Or a plane. Going up and down like this is just how it feels to be in a plane during turbulence. Wouldn't it be lucky if you hit some turbulence during your flight and you could shut your eyes and imagine yourself back here, having this wonderful time on the carousel!"

Joanna booked her flight the next day and had no trouble flying.

Fighting the tiger

Ann, a senior librarian at a university, was approaching retirement when she came to see Pat for help with OCD. She had developed a large number of rituals to combat terrifying thoughts both about her own imminent death and bringing death on others. These thoughts did not occur to her when she was at work, where she was totally focused and confident of her abilities, and she had been able to pursue her career and advance to her senior position without any problems. However, outside work, the rituals, which had started during adolescence, were totally governing her life. They had always stopped her from forming relationships or making close friends and she lived alone. She dreaded giving up work and being left totally in the grip of her demons.

Over the years, Ann had developed whole sequences of actions that she had to carry out to protect herself from being struck dead or from doing unintentional harm to others – these included walking around the very edges of her living room and bedroom, squeezing behind furniture to do so, putting her collection of CDs in a reverse order, walking on tiptoe four times up and downstairs, changing her bed linen, washing it and ironing it, and so on. These rituals took so much time that she was usually up very late and then found herself too wound up to go to sleep. If she did drop off, she awoke quickly in panic. She was convinced she was sleeping less than one hour a night.

> 66 Ann had developed whole sequences of actions to protect herself ... 99

Pat learned that Ann had nearly drowned as a young child, when she fell into a river. As a result, her mother became hugely overly protective of her and refused to let her do anything that might be mildly risky, even riding a bike or climbing trees. Not long afterwards, Ann's father had died very suddenly from a heart attack. This came as a terrible shock to her and her mother became even more anxious on Ann's behalf.

Pat quickly helped Ann restore a good sleep pattern. She also told her how it had been established that people commonly sleep more than they realise and gave her some good sleep hygiene tips. Having explained the importance of dreaming, she then said, "So when we get ready to sleep, we need to point ourselves towards the dream state, rather than towards the day that has gone. You can do that by focusing on your senses – the sounds you can hear in the room, the texture of the bedclothes, the warmth you feel in your body, and so on. Every time you feel yourself straying into a thought, just gently bring your focus back to your physical self. You can even visualise being on a quiet beach, or some other lovely place, and let all your senses revel in being there. Then you are halfway to the dream state."

She encouraged Ann to see the OCD as a stuck circuit – something outside of herself. Another time she described it as a trance state. "It has you spellbound, but you can break the spell. You are bigger than all of those rituals. They can't dictate to *you*." Pat provided Ann with many suggestions of this kind, to help her view OCD as distinct from herself, and Ann found such images very helpful.

At the third session, she reported that her sleep was much

better and, at the fifth, that she had managed to stop herself from performing some of her rituals when the death thoughts came into her head. But she felt she was fighting a hydra-headed monster. Whenever she gained control over one or two of the rituals, several more sprang up to take their place so that, just when she had started to convince herself that she was indeed bigger than the rituals, the new ones would crow, "Oh, no you're not!" And she would believe them again. So Pat continued, week by week, suggesting new ways to perceive the OCD rituals and helping Ann work with those ideas.

In the early stages, Ann was far too fearful to allow herself to relax. So, at first, Pat simply concentrated on telling her jokes to make her laugh and stories to focus her attention. She also taught her the 7/11 breathing technique, however, and gradually Ann learned how to relax herself. One day, after about 15 sessions, Pat told her the following story of the prince and the tiger.

It was the custom in his kingdom for a prince to have to kill a tiger, before he could inherit the throne. His father, the king, told him the time had come and that he must start training to kill the tiger that even now was ready for him in the dungeons. But the prince was so terrified at the very thought that he fled the palace.

He came to the home of a rich landowner and begged to be allowed to stay for a while. The landowner was happy to oblige.

And so the prince stayed there and spent his time walking in the vast grounds, trying to collect his thoughts. Then, one day, he noticed tigers prowling at the edge of the woods that bordered the grounds. Fearfully, he reported this to the landowner, who said, "Oh, yes, they come there a lot. They don't do any harm." In horror, the prince took off again and, after a long day's walking, reached a castle guarded by an old soldier. The soldier took pity on him in his weary state and invited him in to eat with all the young soldiers inside. Soon the prince was very comfortable with them and had just started to relax, when one of the soldiers said, "We are going on a tiger hunt tomorrow! You must come with us!" The prince's blood ran cold with fear but he didn't dare refuse. So the next day, he set out with the others but, as soon as he had a chance, he fled.

> 66 Gradually Ann learnt how to relax herself ... 99

After another long day's walking, he arrived at a palace and begged the vizier who opened the gates to take pity on him. "The king will surely welcome you," said the vizier and, sure enough, he did. He invited the prince to eat and provided him with an elegant bed chamber. Out of the window, the next morning, the prince spied the most beautiful young girl – the king's daughter. She was sitting in the perfect palace gardens, seemingly combing her long flowing hair. The prince found himself impelled to go towards her but, just as he came close, he realised that she was not combing her hair but stroking a tiger, which rested with its head in her lap. The prince nearly ran but forced himself not to, and approached her, his legs like jelly. "You don't have to fear my tiger," she smiled. "He is tame. He protects us. He even prowls the palace at night and tests the doors, to make sure we are safe."

Three nights later, the prince heard a rattle at the door. "It's no good," he said fearfully to himself. "There are tigers everywhere. I might as well go home and face the one I've got to fight, if I am to inherit the kingdom." When he told the king he was leaving, the king said, "Remember me to your father".

"You know my father?"

"Yes, he stayed here once. You look very like him."

The prince set off and, at the end of his first day's journeying, stayed at the castle again. "Remember us to your father," they said. And, when he stayed again with the landowner, the landowner said the same thing.

His father was pleased when the prince told him that he was ready to face the tiger. He had armour brought to him and then the prince descended to the dungeons, where guards released the tiger that was waiting there for him.

The prince was mortally terrified. He raised his sword, ready to strike as the tiger seemed about to leap but, instead, it collapsed on the ground and rolled over, exposing its belly. The prince put away his sword and told his father that he hadn't killed the tiger, as it didn't seem to be a danger.

"Yes, my son. The tiger appeared fierce at first, but, by showing *the necessary courage, you tamed it. You will inherit the kingdom. And, yes, before you ask, I too had to overcome the same fears before I could tame my own tiger."**

As Pat told this story, Ann was clearly deeply engrossed. At the next session, she reported that something amazing had happened to her. She had been lying in bed, once again unable to sleep, swamped by fearful thoughts and the screaming need to defuse them

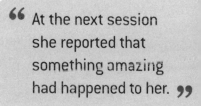

66 At the next session she reported that something amazing had happened to her. **99**

with rituals when, suddenly, something snapped. "I felt utterly furious. I was filled with a blazing energy. I got out of bed, dressed, went into the garden, and shouted out loud with anger. I didn't even care who heard. Then I went back and slept like a log."

"That energy," said Pat, "was the all-powerful life force asserting itself. It is more powerful than any single element in your mind. Nothing can resist it. Certainly not the delinquent thoughts and mechanical parts of your circuitry, which have been so disruptive. The life force has been animating you all your life, whether you knew it or not. And, whenever you can consciously access it, neither the rituals nor the nightmarish thoughts will affect you. They can't."

---

* This is a much shortened retelling of 'The prince who feared tigers' from *Tales from the Bazaars* by Amina Shah (Octagon Press, 2002).

"If you like, you can see it as the force which, in spite of his fear, powered the prince to raise his sword against the tiger."

Ann loved this idea, which experience had already shown her was true. They explored together the (few) times before, when Ann had not even had to struggle but had said a blazing, whole-hearted 'No!' to the rituals, and she recalled how liberated she had felt. Then, through guided imagery, Pat helped her find a place where Ann felt she could tap into that powerful life force. As Ann started to relax, she imagined herself by a beautiful stream with a strong current, which she experienced as the energy of the life force flowing through her. Pat suggested that she could take herself in a split second to that powerful place, whenever she became aroused and fearful, because it was impossible for her essential life force to be browbeaten into performing rituals – in fact, as she'd experienced already, any thought of rituals would disintegrate in that force.

> 66 ... she was clear of both the rituals and the terrifying thoughts. 99

All the many sessions in which they had worked on relaxation and ways to distance Ann from the OCD, and on opening up new perspectives through images and stories, had brought Ann to the point where she could finally tap into and trust her own sense of self. Over the next few weeks, she became stronger and stronger at denying the rituals and eventually became clear of both the rituals and the terrifying thoughts. For the first time she began to think about interesting ways she could spend her retirement and to look forward to studying a new language and taking a course in the history of art, something she'd always wanted to do.

Noises in the night

Sometimes the circumstance that triggers extreme anxiety is not in the past, and therefore cannot be put behind us and moved on from in an ordinary way. People caught up in the 'Troubles' in Northern Ireland, for instance, are in such a position and many have sought support from NOVA, a Barnardo's project that aims to help people traumatised by the conflict. Their important work has shown that even in such cases, there are still powerful ways to help, as the following case history illustrates.

Fourteen-year-old Kenneth had become highly stressed after a sectarian attack with a petrol bomb on his home. His family had endured a catalogue of intimidation and, when they came to NOVA and met Martin, a senior social worker and human givens trained therapist, there was no sense that this was now at an end. Consequently, Kenneth spent most nights unable to sleep, listening out for every noise in case it might signal the start of another attack on his home. He could sleep only during daylight and when other family members were awake. As a result, he had missed a great deal of school, and had been referred to the educational welfare system.

While talking with him, Martin learned of his deep love of music. He listened to it constantly and could identify current chart songs within the first few notes being played. In their work together, there was, of course, no way Martin could offer him reassurances that the intimidation had stopped, or that there would not be another attack on his house. But what he *could* do was help Kenneth to relax. Once he was in a relaxed state, Kenneth was able to realise that the intimidation only ever occurred during the summer holidays, in what is referred to in Northern Ireland as 'the marching season'. And while he was was still deeply relaxed, Martin was also able to help him to appreciate his listening skills, and experience his ability to distinguish between different sounds. He then encouraged him to use those skills to distinguish between the various noises that can be heard at night, when houses are quiet, when they creak and rattle as the heating goes off and they cool down. In this way, the nightly noises could become a reassurance that all was as it should be, rather than a trigger for alarm. He also taught Kenneth simple relaxation exercises to help him get to sleep at the right times.

Martin's work with Kenneth illustrated the importance of establishing small, meaningful goals. As he explains, "When we meet with people in such situations, we must listen to what their goals are, as expressed by them in terms of what it would mean for things to be better. For Kenneth, it meant enjoying a full night's sleep and returning to school again on a regular basis, so that he could pursue his ambitions to go to technical college and at the same time become reconnected with his friends.

"Even in the most tragic of stories, people can express their ideas of what would be positive change through what seem the most ordinary of events. The father whose son was murdered, who simply wanted to be able to read his newspaper or watch the news without crying, or his wife who wanted to be more patient with her grandchildren. Or the young woman who witnessed a gun

> 66 These are all proof that life can improve again, even in the most tragic of circumstances ... 99

and bomb attack at her father's pub, who wanted to be able to meet with her friends for coffee in town without wondering when she would see the gunmen again. Or the young man who, having lost his two older brothers through a sectarian shooting, wanted to find the confidence to complete his work training.

"All of these can be seen as symptomatic of a deeper grief or difficulty, and they are. But, importantly, they are also what each person perceives as potential proof that life can improve again. In supporting them to achieve these goals, by encouraging them to recognise and use their own resources to do so and by reinforcing their ownership of the skills employed, we can help individuals to create and sustain positive changes in life, even in a society where conflict is not yet concluded."*

Seize the moment

We hope this book has inspired you to start taking the necessary steps to deal with unproductive and crippling anxiety. Whatever your circumstances, something can be done. You will no doubt have realised by now that, apart from PTSD-generated anxiety, excessive anxiety arises from unintentional, but excessive, misuse of the imagination, which in turn arises because important needs are not being met in a person's life or their innate resources are being used inefficiently, albeit unwittingly.

Remember too, that anxiety developed (through the fight-or-flight mechanism) as a tool to help us protect ourselves from danger (i.e. by taking action *now*) and so is there to help us, not hinder us. Yet most out-of-control anxiety takes the form of catastrophic imaginings that concern the future or relentless negative ruminating on the possible consequences of what has passed and cannot be altered. You can't be anx-

---

* This story and quotation is taken from 'The trauma goes on', a powerful article by Martin Murphy that was published in the *Human Givens* Journal, 8, 1, 38–41.

ious unless you are fantasising about what is in the future – even if it's only five minutes ahead.

Incapacitating anxiety stops us from truly living, from deeply enjoying our family and friends, from reaching our potential, from fully sharing and caring for others, and challenging ourselves. It makes us selfish and inward looking, miserable and afraid. No one wants to be like this and no one ends up in its grip intentionally. But you *can* take back control, and you now know how. It does take effort and it does take determination. But we have seen people do it many times. The explanations and understandings and the techniques and exercises that we have described in this book, as well as professional help based on human givens ideas, have enabled thousands of people to overcome anxiety and to take the first steps that put real meaning back into their life. They can help *you* too.

> 66 You can take back control ..., and now you know how. 99

*   *   *   *   *

If you have found this book helpful, you might
like to recommend it to friends or colleagues
who could benefit from reading it too.

It's available through all good book shops or
direct from HG Publishing on 01323 811662
or online at: **www.humangivens.com**

INDEX

PRAISE FOR THE AUTHORS' PREVIOUS BOOKS:

How to lift depression... *fast*

"An empowering book ... immediately useful ... Read, use, enjoy and reap the benefits for yourself and others." *Ruth Morozzo, 'Footnotes' Journal*

"As a GP I see many people suffering from depression, and have searched for many years for a good book to recommend to them. At last I have found one. This book draws together the most effective methods from many different approaches to treatment, yet is written in a style which makes the ideas easy to understand and put into practice. The 'human givens' approach detailed in this book is a major step forward in helping people suffering from depression and other mental health problems." *Dr Gina Johnson*

"At last some concrete practical advice. This book offers some real solutions and insight into depression. I can't recommend it enough. If you are suffering from depression or you are caring or treating anyone with this condition, this book will be indispensible. I have spent a lot of money and time researching depression and can say this is without doubt the best book I have read on the subject – I urge you to buy it." *Amazon Review*

"This book is the first I have come across on the subject of depression that is easy to read and understand for both professionals and lay people. It will prove an invaluable resource... The title cover carries the phrase 'Change is much easier than you think' and that theme flows throughout the book. [It] offers readers much practical help and advice ... a book for every library and one that should not sit on the shelf and gather dust." *'Professional Social Work' Magazine*

"Everyone involved in administering personal therapy should read this book." *Nursing Standard*

How to lift depression... fast is published in paperback by HG Publishing (2006) ISBN: 1-899398-41-4

Freedom from Addiction:
The secret behind successful addiction busting

"Following *How to Lift Depression...fast* this second title is highly recommended. It sidesteps jargon, avoids the medicalisation of addictive behaviour, explodes the lies that maintain addiction and offers realistic, practical solutions."
Peter Barraclough, Nursing Standard

"So many books promise so much, and then fail to deliver. This book is of an entirely different quality. If you have an addiction/compulsive behaviour, do yourself a big favour, buy it – it gives answers ... a big thankyou to the authors." *Amazon Review*

"An easy-to-read, empowering self-help guide for those considering themselves 'addicted' to anything... It breaks down simply the self-assessment needed for discerning problem areas and their development, adding relevant research in a jargon-free manner; with a fascinating explanation for how neurophysiology and 'pattern-matching' underpin symptoms like craving."
Neia Glynn, The Psychologist

"Here is another excellent book from that groundbreaking team, Joe Griffin and Ivan Tyrrell. This time the focus is on addiction, how it comes about, and a highly effective way of dealing with it – whether it be a life threatening addiction (and many are) or an annoying habit which one would like to be rid of... There are techniques and ways of looking at problems which we can assimilate and pass on to our clients. *Freedom from Addiction* is easy to read, gives clear guidance and is an ideal book to have to hand to enable you to help yourself, your family, your friends and your clients." *Ruth Morozzo, 'Footnotes' Journal*

"Full of insights, this book is truly superb, not just in the area of understanding and managing addictions but also in providing a broader, clear, coherent and wholly convincing insight into human thought processes and behaviours. " *Amazon Review*

Freedom from Addiction is published in paperback
by HG Publishing (2005) ISBN: 1-899398-46-5

Human Givens:
A new approach to emotional health and clear thinking

"*Human Givens* is the most practical and intuitive book I've read in years." *Charles Hayes, Autodidactic Press, USA*

"Harnessed between these pages are scientific insights and practical techniques of sufficient power to completely revolutionise our approach to parenting, teaching and the caring professions. I wholeheartedly recommend *Human Givens* to any individual with a burning interest in how life works and can be helped to work better." *Dr Nick Baylis, University of Cambridge's Well-being Institute*

"Griffin and Tyrrell's contribution advances psychology as much as the introduction of the Arabic numeric system with its zero digit advanced mathematics." *Washington Times*

"A quiet revolution." *New Scientist*   "Key insights." *Financial Times*

"Important original work ... both aesthetically pleasing and of immense practical use... has great relevance to all areas of life... could save (tax payers) millions of pounds. " *Dr Farouk Okhai, Consultant Psychiatrist in Psychotherapy*

"A wonderfully fresh and stimulating view of dreaming, evolution, and human functioning. *Human Givens* also provides both an encompassing model and practical, specific applications to enhance the effectiveness of psychotherapy. It will deepen and widen every reader's perspective." *Arthur J. Deikman, M.D., Clinical Professor of Psychiatry, University of California*

"In *Human Givens* Griffin and Tyrrell offer innovative perspectives on promoting effective living. They have synthesized brain and social research in such a way that they provide new templates for understanding how to unlock the best in human nature." *Dr Jeffrey K. Zeig, Director of the Milton H. Erickson Foundation*

"While books are never a cure for what ails us in life, they are often a catalyst, a trigger that fires off those rare and profound 'aha!' moments that lead to deeper insights and understanding. *Human Givens* is such a catalyst." *Jack Davies*

Human Givens is published in paperback
by HG Publishing (2004) ISBN: 1-899398-31-7

Dreaming Reality:
How dreaming keeps us sane or can drive us mad

"*Dreaming Reality* exquisitely scythes through the Gordian knot created by past dream theories. Even better, like all the very best explanations, its central theme is as far-reaching as it is intuitive. Through a fascinating combination of dream examples and scientific findings, it provides lucid and compelling evidence for how our night and daydreams not only mould our personalities but also lie at the very heart of being human." *Dr Clive Bromhall, author of 'The Eternal Child'*

"A remarkable book that makes compelling reading. Griffin and Tyrrell's adroitly written text challenges traditional views on our knowledge and understanding of the mystifying covert world of dreams." *Professor Tony Charlton, Professor of Behavioural Studies, University of Gloucestershire*

"This book is revolutionary in more than one way. Past and sometimes overlooked research is re-evaluated, and a persuasive theory emerges... long overdue to my mind." *Doris Lessing*

"For anyone who has speculated on the meaning and purpose of dreaming, Griffin and Tyrrell's astounding insights light up the dark corners of the mind. Not since 1964 when Carl Jung's book *Man and his Symbols* was published has anyone set out to write so conclusively on dreaming for a wide audience.

Griffin and Tyrrell [propose] that dreaming functions to cleanse the undischarged emotional arousals of the day and they explain how this happens through metaphorical pattern-matching. From this one sets off on the journey to understanding the true causes of (and routes to healing) depression.

This book is revolutionary in thought, revelatory in content and will be established as the most important twenty-first century milestone on the road to accessible mental health treatment for all. It's a must for all who live with mental illness or work for its relief." *Ian Hunter* OBE

Dreaming Reality: How dreaming keeps us sane, or can drive us mad is published in paperback by HG Publishing (2006) ISBN: 1-899398-91-0

Further information

To find your nearest human givens therapist in private practice, visit: **www.hgi.org.uk/register**

For details about other books and audio CDs published by HG Publishing, visit:
www.humangivens.com

For more information about the human givens approach, including articles and case histories, visit the Human Givens Institute's website at:
www.hgi.org.uk

For details of courses visit:
www.humangivenscollege.com